WRITING SKILLS CURRICULUM LIBRARY

Ready-to-Use
PARAGRAPH
WRITING
Activities

UNIT 3

JACK UMSTATTER

Illustrations by Maureen Umstatter

JOSSEY-BASS
A Wiley Imprint
www.josseybass.com

Published by Jossey-Bass
A Wiley Imprint
989 Market Street, San Francisco, CA 94103-1741   www.josseybass.com

Jossey-Bass books and products are available through most bookstores. To contact Jossey-Bass directly call our Customer Care Department within the U.S. at 800-956-7739, outside the U.S. at 317-572-3986 or fax 317-572-4002.

Jossey-Bass also publishes its books in a variety of electronic formats. Some content that appears in print may not be available in electronic books.

Library of Congress Cataloging-in-Publication Data

Umstatter, Jack.
    Writing skills curriculum library / Umstatter, Jack.
        p.   cm.
    Contents: Unit 3. Ready-to-use Paragraph Writing Activities
    ISBN 0-87628-484-5
    1. English language—Composition and exercises—Study and teaching
(Secondary)—United States.   2. Education, Secondary—Activity
programs—United States.   I. Title.
    LB1631.U49   1999
    808'.042'0712—dc21   99-21556
                                                                              CIP

FIRST EDITION
PB Printing 10 9 8 7 6

DEDICATED

To Maureen Umstatter, my daughter, for her love, joie de vivre,
and for all the times we, as a family, have been (and continue to be) proud of you.

ACKNOWLEDGMENTS

Thanks to my daughter Maureen for her artistic creativity and to my wife Chris for her many hours of work on this project. I couldn't have done it without you.

Thanks again to Connie Kallback and Win Huppuch for their support and encouragement with this series.

Appreciation and thanks to Diane Turso for her meticulous development and copyediting and to Mariann Hutlak, production editor, for her tireless attention throughout the project.

To John Tessitore, a former student and current biographer and magazine writer, thanks for his writings featured in Activities 3–69 and 3–75.

Thanks to two other former students, Aaron Bronfman (Activity 3–70) and Meredith McCloskey (Activity 3–72) for their writings.

A special thanks to my students, past and present, who inspire these ideas and activities.

Thanks to Terry from WISCO COMPUTING of Wisconsin Rapids, Wisconsin 54495 for his programs.

Definitions for certain words are taken from *Webster's New World Dictionary, Third College Edition* (New York: Simon & Schuster, Inc., 1988).

ABOUT THE AUTHOR

Jack Umstatter has taught English on both the junior high and senior high school levels since 1972, and education and literature at Dowling College (Oakdale, New York) for the past nine years. He currently teaches English in the Cold Spring Harbor School District in New York.

Mr. Umstatter graduated from Manhattan College with a B.A. in English and completed his M.A. in English at S.U.N.Y.—Stony Brook. He earned his Educational Administration degree at Long Island University.

Mr. Umstatter has been selected Teacher of the Year several times and was elected to *Who's Who Among America's Teachers*. Most recently, he appeared in *Contemporary Authors*. Mr. Umstatter has taught all levels of secondary English classes including the Honors and Advanced Placement classes. As coach of the high school's Academic team, the Brainstormers, he led the team in capturing the Long Island and New York State championships when competing in the American Scholastic Competition Network National Tournament of Champions in Lake Forest, Illinois.

Mr. Umstatter's other publications include *Hooked on Literature!* (1994), *201 Ready-to-Use Word Games for the English Classroom* (1994), *Brain Games!* (1996), and *Hooked on English!* (1997), all published by The Center for Applied Research in Education.

ABOUT THE WRITING SKILLS CURRICULUM LIBRARY

According to William Faulkner, a writer needs three things—experience, observation, and imagination. As teachers, we know that our students certainly have these essentials. Adolescents love to express themselves in different ways. Writing is undoubtedly one of these modes of expression. We stand before potential novelists, poets, playwrights, columnists, essayists, and satirists (no comment!). How to tap these possibilities is our task.

The six-unit *Writing Skills Curriculum Library* was created to help your students learn the elements of effective writing and enjoy the experience at the same time. This series of progressive, reproducible activities will instruct your students in the various elements of the writing process as it fosters an appreciation for the writing craft. These stimulating and creative activities also serve as skill reinforcement tools. Additionally, since the lesson preparation has already been done, you will be able to concentrate on guiding your students instead of having to create, develop, and sequence writing exercises.

- Unit 1, *Ready-to-Use Word Activities*, concentrates on the importance of word selection and exactness in the writing process. William Somerset Maugham said, "Words have weight, sound, and appearance; it is only by considering these that you can write a sentence that is good to look at and good to listen to." Activities featuring connotations, denotations, prefixes, roots, suffixes, synonyms, antonyms, and expressions will assist your students in becoming more conscientious and selective "verbivores," as Richard Lederer would call them. Diction, syntax, and specificity are also emphasized here.

- The renowned essayist, philosopher, and poet, Ralph Waldo Emerson, commented on the necessity of writing effective sentences. He said, "For a few golden sentences we will turn over and actually read a volume of four or five hundred pages." Knowing the essentials of the cogent sentence is the focus of Unit 2, *Ready-to-Use Sentence Activities*. Here a thorough examination of subjects, predicates, complements, types of sentences, phrases, clauses, punctuation, capitalization, and agreement situations can be found. Problems including faulty subordination, wordiness, split infinitives, dangling modifiers, faulty transition, and ambiguity are also addressed within these activities.

- "Every man speaks and writes with the intent to be understood." Samuel Johnson obviously recognized the essence of an effective paragraph. Unit 3, *Ready-to-Use Paragraph Writing Activities*, leads the students through the steps of writing clear, convincing paragraphs. Starting with brainstorming techniques, these activities also emphasize the importance of developing effective thesis statements and topic sentences, selecting an appropriate paragraph form, organizing the paragraph, introducing the paragraph, utilizing relevant supporting ideas, and concluding the paragraph. Activities focusing on methods of developing a topic—description, exemplification, process, cause and effect, comparison-contrast, analogy, persuasion, and definition—are included.

- "General and abstract ideas are the source of the greatest errors of mankind." Jean-Jacques Rousseau's words befit Unit 4, *Ready-to-Use Prewriting & Organization Activities*, for here the emphasis is on gathering and using information intelligently. Activities include sources of information, categorization, topics and sub-topics, summaries, outlines, details, thesis statements, term paper ideas, and formats.

- "Most people won't realize that writing is a craft." Katherine Anne Porter's words could be the fifth unit's title. Unit 5, *Ready-to-Use Revision & Proofreading Activities*, guides the students through the problem areas of writing. Troublesome areas such as verb tense, words often confused, superfluity, double negatives, and clarity issues are presented in interesting and innovative ways. Students will become better proofreaders as they learn to utilize the same methods used by professional writers.

- "Our appreciation of fine writing will always be in proportion to its real difficulty and its apparent ease." Charles Caleb Colton must have been listening in as Unit 6, *Ready-to-Use Portfolio Development Activities*, was developed. Students are exposed to many different types of practical writings including literary analyses, original stories and sketches, narratives, reviews, letters, journal entries, newspaper articles, character analyses, dialogue writing, college admission essays, and commercials. The goal is to make the difficult appear easy!

Whether you use these realistic classroom-tested activities for introduction, remediation, reinforcement, or enrichment, they will guide your students toward more effective writing. Many of the activities include riddles, hidden words and sayings, word-finds, and other devices that allow students to check their own answers. These activities will also help you to assess your students' progress.

So go ahead and make Mr. Faulkner proud by awakening the experience, observation, and imagination of your students. The benefits will be both theirs—and yours!

Jack Umstatter

ABOUT UNIT 3

Ready-to-Use Paragraph Writing Activities, the third unit in the *Writing Skills Curriculum Library*, includes 90 creative, practical, and reproducible activities that guide students through the paragraph development process. Whether you choose to use an activity as an introduction, a reinforcement, a homework assignment, a test or quiz, research, or as remediation, your students will enjoy themselves and learn at the same time. Some of the activities can be used as a 10- or 15-minute segment in class, while others can be used for the entire period. They are useful as an individual, small group/cooperative learning, or entire-class activity. Some of the activities use riddles, hidden words, sayings, quotations, word-finds, and other devices that all allow students to check their own answers.

- Activities 3–1 through 3–17, "Starting Up," present the basics of the writing process. Here students will review the parts of speech, the components of a complete sentence, and punctuation. Additionally, six activities focus on proofreading, an important part of students' writing.

- Activities 3–18 through 3–30, "Becoming More Efficient," focus on writing effective sentences. Developing clear, concise sentences and then combining sentences using strong transitions are covered here. Four activities designed to help students distinguish between facts and opinions, a necessary step in writing strong thesis statements and topic sentences, are also in this section.

- Activities 3–31 through 3–46, "Generating Ideas," deal with brainstorming a topic, creating intelligent thesis statements and topic sentences, and supporting those ideas using convincing evidence. Through these activities your students will become more capable and confident in their argumentation.

- Activities 3–47 through 3–60, "Zeroing In," are a potpourri of writers' tools. Paraphrasing, writing illustrative sentences, and using the most appropriate words are covered in an interesting fashion. Several fun activities featuring oxymorons, eponyms, and idioms are also in this section.

- Activities 3–61 through 3–75, "Developing Skills," allow the students to examine specific types of academic writings. These writings include descriptions, reports, and interviews. Additionally, the analogy essay, the comparison–contrast essay, the cause-and-effect essay, the persuasive essay, the narrative essay, the classification essay, and the definition essay are taught and exemplified here.

- Activities 3–76 through 3–90, "Imagining Things," are enjoyable writing activities. Focusing on skill development and writing enjoyment, students write about themselves, other people, interesting situations, and memorable places. Whether it be imagining themselves as a teen in the past or in the future, taking on the persona of an advice columnist, or describing a friend, your writers will improve their skills and have a good time doing so.

These classroom-tested ready-to-use activities will allow you to better utilize your time and skills as a writing facilitator. They will also help your students become better writers who look forward to expressing themselves more skillfully and confidently. It is a winning combination! Enjoy!

Jack Umstatter

CONTENTS

SECTION ONE
STARTING UP

SECTION TWO
BECOMING MORE EFFICIENT

SECTION THREE
GENERATING IDEAS

SECTION FOUR
ZEROING IN

SECTION FIVE
DEVELOPING SKILLS

SECTION SIX
IMAGINING THINGS

TEACHER'S CORRECTION MARKS

ab	abbreviation problem
agr	agreement problem
amb	ambiguous
awk	awkward expression or construction
cap	capitalize
case	error in case
cp	comma problem
cs	comma splice
d	inappropriate diction
det	details are needed
dm	dangling modifier
dn	double negative
frag	fragment
ital	italics or underline
lc	use lower case
mm	misplaced modifier
num	numbers problem
^	insert
¶	new paragraph needed
‖	faulty parallelism
,	insert comma
pass	misuse of passive voice

pr ref	pronoun reference problem
pun	punctuation needed or missing
reas	reasoning needs improvement
rep	unnecessary repetition
RO	run-on
shift	faulty tense shift
sp	incorrect spelling
thesis	improve the thesis
trans	improve the transition
TX	topic sentence needed (or improved)
U	usage problem
UW	unclear wording
V	variety needed
VAG	vague
VE	verb error
VT	verb tense problem
w	wordy
WC	better word choice
WM	word missing
WW	wrong word

SECTION ONE

STARTING UP

3-1. IDENTIFYING THE PARTS OF SPEECH

On the line below each sentence, write the part of speech for each word in the sentence. Use the following abbreviations: **adj** for adjective, **adv** for adverb, **c** for conjunction, **i** for interjection, **n** for noun, **p** for pronoun, **prep** for preposition, and **v** for verb.

1. Each of the participants felt nervous before the important event.

   _____

2. How can I describe the exhilarating feeling it gave me?

   _____

3. Both of you should consider the options before you lease this automobile.

   _____

4. "Read this and give me a report soon," the boss demanded of his worker.

   _____

5. The speaker was annoyed by the incessant chattering in the room.

   _____

6. I will accomplish the task shortly.

   _____

7. Neither Jesse nor his helpers could lift this heavy object.

   _____

8. I do not believe this store stays open after six o'clock.

   _____

9. Carry yourself with great dignity as you walk carefully down the aisle.

   _____

10. It seems to me that the very best players from our league were selected.

   _____

3-2. PARTS-OF-SPEECH REVIEW

On the line below each sentence, write the abbreviation of each word's part of speech. Write **adj** for adjective, **adv** for adverb, **c** for conjunction, **i** for interjection, **n** for noun, **p** for pronoun, **prep** for preposition, and **v** for verb.

1. He went to the store.

_____

2. May we see your car?

_____

3. Rock me gently.

_____

4. You can not start a fire.

_____

5. Bertha and I walked six miles.

_____

6. Hey! That lamp is falling.

_____

7. The road is slippery and windy.

_____

8. Will you and I ever be friends again?

_____

9. Hit the ball.

_____

10. Because I am tired, I will go to bed now.

_____

11. She brushed her teeth and combed her hair.

_____

12. How am I driving?

_____

3-3. PARTS-OF-SPEECH REVIEW CROSSWORD PUZZLE

Using the sentence, **"Usually Theresa and Regina, who are our current officers, announce the events of the day on the microphone located in the large office,"** answer the clues all dealing with that sentence. Fill in the appropriate spaces in the crossword puzzle.

ACROSS

1. an adverb
5. the last word in the first prepositional phrase
6. last preposition in the sentence
7. first proper noun in the sentence
10. acts as a pronoun and an adjective
11. the number of common nouns
12. the second preposition in the sentence
10. a word that is a pronoun/adjective
13. a predicate noun
14. a relative pronoun
15. the sentence's last adjective
17. the word *current* is a(n) _____

DOWN

2. a male's name that can be formed by rearranging the letters of the noun *events*
3. the first verb in the sentence
4. a participle
7. an article
8. the sentence's main verb
9. the last word of the second prepositional phrase
10. the last common noun in the sentence
16. a conjunction

3-4. PLACING THE PUNCTUATION MARKS IN THEIR PROPER PLACES

These 10 sentences contain no punctuation. Using apostrophes, colons, commas, dashes, exclamation marks, periods, question marks, quotation marks, and semicolons, correctly punctuate these sentences. Each punctuation mark will be used at least once.

1. This is the first day of the rest of your life a wise man once told me

_____

_____

2. What do you intend to do with your future he asked me

_____

_____

3. Though some think life is a chore you should not

_____

_____

4. Theres so much to do each day life is a present to be enjoyed

_____

_____

5. Many people do not realize how precious life is

_____

_____

6. Some others live by the proverb lifes moments are momentous

_____

_____

7. Life is shall I say a beautiful experience

_____

_____

8. The wise man then made this statement I have lived my life to the fullest

_____

_____

9. What have I taught you the wise man asked me before he left

_____

_____

10. Carpe diem I exclaimed

_____

_____

Name _____ Date _____ Period _____

3-5. REVIEWING PUNCTUATION MARKS

Match each punctuation mark in Column A with its function in Column B. Then, on the reverse side of this paper, write 10 sentences, each one illustrating a different punctuation mark.

Column A

1. ____ apostrophe [']

2. ____ colon [:]

3. ____ comma [,]

4. ____ dash [—]

5. ____ exclamation mark [!]

6. ____ parentheses [( )]

7. ____ period [.]

8. ____ question mark [?]

9. ____ quotation marks [" "]

10. ____ semicolon [;]

Column B

A. to indicate an abrupt change in thought or a break in the sentence flow

B. after a declarative sentence and most imperative sentences

C. to enclose titles of poems, essays, short stories, and chapters of books

D. between independent clauses not joined by a coordinating conjunction

E. to show the possessive case of nouns and certain pronouns

F. after a particularly forceful interjection or imperative sentence

G. to enclose material that is explanatory, supplementary, or exemplifying

H. after direct questions

I. to separate an introductory clause or phrase from the main clause

J. to introduce a formal statement, a long quotation, or a speech in a play

3-6. JUMBLED SENTENCES

The order of the words in each sentence below is scrambled. Write the words in the correct order on the line below the scrambled version. The capitalized letter is the sentence's first word.

1. the The crossed street chicken.

   _____

2. her recordings listened to Nancy.

   _____

3. sang assembly the for choir Our.

   _____

4. down pushed She car's brake on the.

   _____

5. in the joy life my Bring back.

   _____

6. is no frigate book a like There.

   _____

7. hired was Sharon restructure the committee to.

   _____

8. home us They back welcomed.

   _____

9. your store location What exact the is of?

   _____

10. true good to is too be This!

    _____

11. difficult It perfect score to very is have a.

    _____

12. I am with to be glad birthday your on you.

    _____

© 1999 by John Wiley & Sons, Inc.

3-7. TURNING FRAGMENTS INTO SENTENCES

These 15 groups of words are all fragments. Using all the words in each original group and keeping them in their present order, add words to the fragment to form a complete sentence. Write your answers on the lines below the groups of words.

1. into the toughest part of the course _____

_____

2. running the Chicago Marathon next month _____

_____

3. whenever the clock approached midnight _____

_____

4. borrowed from the elderly man down the street _____

_____

5. while he checked the motorist's license _____

_____

6. off at school next Tuesday _____

_____

7. the piccolo player who auditioned _____

_____

8. the beautiful portrait drawn by Maureen _____

_____

9. gracefully dancing _____

_____

10. Helen found that talking to _____

_____

11. did _____

_____

12. talking to her niece _____

_____

13. I will never understand why some people _____

_____

14. the costume that Kate wore that Halloween _____

_____

15. in the corner of our yard _____

_____

3-8. HOW TASTY!

There are five phrases, five clauses, and five sentences in the 15 groups of words below. Write the letter **P** if the group of words is a phrase, **C** if it is a clause, and **S** if it is a sentence. The first words are purposely capitalized. Then, on the appropriate lines below the last question, write the corresponding two letters, in order, for the phrase, the clause, and the sentence. If your answers are correct, you will spell out three words that will make this activity's title make sense!

1. _____ (SW) That he intended to purchase.

2. _____ (AR) Growing up in the South.

3. _____ (SA) Their reasons certainly make sense to me.

4. _____ (EE) Which the group selected.

5. _____ (TI) Without a prayer.

6. _____ (CC) Can you recall the last time we heard such uplifting news?

7. _____ (HA) Send it along.

8. _____ (FI) To remember the name of his workers

9. _____ (TE) Who was our favorite singer

10. _____ (RI) If he is that interested in the position, mail him an application.

11. _____ (CI) By the window next to Stu's desk

12. _____ (NE) Unless the wind changes soon.

13. _____ (RS) Because you were more qualified than he.

14. _____ (NE) He would usually rent the ski house for his employees.

15. _____ (AL) Lifting the heavy box by himself.

The phrases spell out the word _____. The clauses spell out the word

_____. The sentences spell out the word _____.

3-9. EACH HAS 40

There are five sentences, five fragments, and five run-ons in these 15 groups of words. In the appropriate spaces, write **S** for sentence, **F** for fragment, and **RO** for run-on. Then add up the answer numbers for each of the three. Thus, since the first answer is a sentence (S), the sentence category now has a total of one. Do the same with the remaining 14 groups of words. If your 15 answers are correct, the sentence, the fragment, and the run-on will each total 40!

1. _____   There is nothing wrong with that way of thinking.

2. _____   Catch the waves, they are really beautiful today.

3. _____   In the middle of the road with other bicyclists.

4. _____   Let's eat here, the food is always quite tasty.

5. _____   You and I against the rest of them.

6. _____   The judge did not rule on our situation yet.

7. _____   Lance Butler, the woman's attorney, returned briefly to the courthouse.

8. _____   Had subpoenaed them two days ago.

9. _____   He was a vocal exile leader, he spoke up for the rights of his people.

10. _____   Distance learning could replace traditional classroom teaching, this is an interesting statement.

11. _____   According to many of the people closely associated with the president.

12. _____   Many interesting classes have already been offered.

13. _____   Taking in all could read during that short time.

14. _____   Clearly these are all responsible people.

15. _____   The problem is the same with both cars, their transmissions need work.

Name _____ Date _____ Period _____

3-10. MISTAKES...MISTAKES...MISTAKES

On the line below each sentence, write the group of words so that it is a completely correct sentence. You may have to add or rearrange words for some of them.

1. I ain't tired.

   _____

2. He eaten a pretzel during the concert.

   _____

3. She is the tallest of the two Thompson sisters.

   _____

4. You and him are the champions of the tournament.

   _____

5. He brung it here to our house yesterday.

   _____

6. Are they goin home know?

   _____

7. Don't they rember hour house number?

   _____

8. Gina, this problem about cheating on the test is the difficultest one of all.

   _____

9. Down by the largest mall in the state.

   _____

10. Their is no such thing!

    _____

11. Josie is our chosen leader, we listen to her.

    _____

12. Some of the pepperoni pizza have been ate.

    _____

13. One of the students are selected to be chairperson each month.

    _____

14. Wedesday is her favoritte day of the week.

    _____

15. Stop this racket imediately!

    _____

3-11. 13 ERRORS

There are 13 errors contained in this paragraph. These errors could include misspellings, fragments, run-ons, as well as mistakes in grammar and usage. On the appropriate lines following this paragraph, correct these 13 mistakes. The first one is done for you. Not every numbered group of words has a mistake; however, a group may have more than one error.

(1) We had heard the reports of the hurricane for the passed three days. (2) As it blew by Puerto Rico, it was picking up more speed. (3) With winds nearing one hundred fifteen miles per hour. (4) Two years ago those folks who live on the Outer Banks of North Carolina had already experienced, two frightening hurricanes—within two months of each other. (5) Needless to say, most residents, having lost much twenty four months earlier, heeded the warnings of weather fourcasters and evacuated inland. (6) The people along the Atlantic Coast listened intently to the hurricane reports. (7) Local beach officials did not permit swimming. (8) Though surfing was allowed in some areas. (9) Tides were exceptionally high waves; were three to six feel above normal. (10) The water was up to the dunes and boardwalks two days before the hurricane even hit the mainland hundred of miles away. (11) The lessons teached by any hurricane is quite simple. (12) Safety is paramour. (13) Those who throw caution to the wind might not live to tell about the next hurricane.

1. past _____

2. _____

3. _____

4. _____

5. _____

6. _____

7. _____

8. _____

9. _____

10. _____

11. _____

12. _____

13. _____

3-12. THE BACKYARD EXPERIENCE

The following paragraph needs many corrections. There are fragments, run-ons, misspellings, word omissions, and punctuation errors. On the lines below the original paragraph, write the corrected form.

While I sit in my backyard. I can hear the neighbors. Playing in their swimming pool. The young boys, Danny and Phil, are my neighbor's nephews. They are playing games. Such as Wave Pool, Marco Polo, Hold Your Breath and Find the Coin. Danny's father, Robert, is also playing, he does not try very hard because he wants his sons to win. Danny has hurt his hand. When he tagged his dad during the game of Tag. He is crying and his father trying to comfort him. Is not very effective. So Danny leaves the pool and decides to eat. Hamburgers and hot dogs. Phil, the younger brother, and his dad also leave the pool to eat. Because they are hungry after playing in the pool for over an hour. The rest of the relatives are enjoying their supper. And invite me over to join them. I politely refuse. Saying I am going to eat my supper with my wife and children. In a few minutes.

_____

_____

_____

_____

_____

_____

_____

_____

_____

_____

_____

_____

_____

_____

3-13. THE PARAGRAPH THAT NEEDS MUCH WORK

There are numerous mistakes within this paragraph. There are errors in spelling, punctuation, capitalization, plurals, usage, agreement, idioms, word omission, and more. Correct these errors by rewriting the paragraph on the lines provided for you. (Use the back of this sheet if you need more space.) Discuss your answers with your classmates.

The last time I seen Juan he is waving good-bye from the plain taking him to his nature Spain. Juan had had lived with a family in hour town when he was an eschange student too years ago. He was in my Social studies class and we struck up an imediate friendship. Both of us likes the same kind of music and we were starters in the soccer team that one the county championship. Seldom homesick Juan adopted well to our countries customs. He felled in love with the many intranational resterrants in the city only thirty minutes away, from us. Wanting to be a traveling journalism Juan took as several language courses, and spoke with many peoples hopping to become more, fluent in the language. Assuredly he will become a succes in his chosen field, because he works so diligent. I hope to visit Juan and his family in Madrid this Summer.

_____

_____

_____

_____

_____

_____

_____

_____

_____

_____

_____

_____

_____

_____

_____

3-14. THE ERROR DETECTOR

Each sentence contains an error. Match the sentence from Column A with its error in Column B by writing the corresponding letter in the space next to the number. If your answers are correct, you will spell out a three-letter verb, a four-letter adjective, and a three-letter boy's first name. Write those words in the appropriate spaces at the bottom of this page.

Column A

1. ____ Bob and me went to the store.
2. ____ She had drank two glasses of water before supper last night.
3. ____ The mechanic fixed my car, the bill was three hundred dollars.
4. ____ Each of the costumes have buttons missing.
5. ____ My nefew will be visiting us this summer.
6. ____ "I would like to help the flood victims", Joe said.
7. ____ The boat was moving at fifteen nots per hour.
8. ____ We will resume our conversation later I have to pick up my uncle at the station now.
9. ____ Leaving the museum with his second grade class.
10. ____ Three deers were spotted in the park last night.
11. ____ Eating at the restaurant, the fork was lifted by Dad.
12. ____ Everyone had their umbrella at the concert.
13. ____ After the exciting movie was over we walked home by ourselves.

Column B

A. incorrect comma placement
B. wrong verb tense
C. misplaced modifier
D. wrong word
E. comma splice
F. pronoun and antecedent number problem
G. error in subject–verb agreement
H. comma is needed after an introductory adverbial clause
 I. fragment
 J. run-on
K. wrong case for the sentence's subject
L. misspelling
M. incorrect plural form of the word

The verb is _____; the adjective is _____; the boy's name

is _____.

3-15. MATCHING ERRORS AND EXAMPLES

Seventeen sentences illustrating common mechanical errors are found below. Write the letter of the common mistake found in Group B next to its corresponding example in Group A. If you answer all 17 correctly, the letters will spell out, in order, three nouns and a common abbreviation. Write those three words and the abbreviation at the bottom of this page.

Group A

1. ____ The convention was held in montreal.
2. ____ In the middle of the concert.
3. ____ He walked slow down the hallway.
4. ____ This is the quickest way to the stadium, follow me.
5. ____ The family enjoys visiting exotic places, photographing animals, and art work.
6. ____ Is it possible to locate thier new home?
7. ____ Each of these passengers are welcome to stay with the group.
8. ____ Kevin was as busy as a bee.
9. ____ Wandering aimlessly through the museum, the sculpture was seen by my sister.
10. ____ Are you traveling with Joe's crew tomorrow.
11. ____ We ain't gonna stand for it again.
12. ____ The children were digging a huge whole in the sand.
13. ____ All the doughnuts had been ate before you arrived.
14. ____ This is the familys' decision.
15. ____ We went school to see our favorite teacher, Miss McPhee.
16. ____ Before the trip we will talked to the guide.
17. ____ Have you read Huxley's Brave New World yet?

Group B

A. misuse of the adverb
C. wrong word
D. use italics, bold letters, or underline
E. correct the apostrophe
F. add a needed word
G. capitalization problem
H. irregular verb problem
I. faulty parallelism
L. misplaced modifier
M. verb tense problem
O. punctuation problem
P. cliché
R. fragment
T. misspelling
V. run-on
W. slang
Y. subject–verb agreement problem

Write the answer letters (in order) here _____.

These letters spell out the words _____, _____,

_____, and the abbreviation _____.

3-16. BY THE NUMBERS

Robert was asked to compose 15 different sentences. One requirement was that the sentence had to have the same number of words as the sentence's number. Thus, the group of words in number six should consist of six words. Though he tried hard, Robert did not succeed because only five of these 15 groups of words are sentences. Circle the numbers of the five groups of words that are sentences.

1. Now.

2. Break it.

3. They are here.

4. I am, you are.

5. Looking at the helicopter land.

6. Steve wondered why this was occurring.

7. A policeman pulled up, we were surprised.

8. We spent the day walking through the town.

9. The compelling new series that will start next week.

10. Our company spends thousands of dollars on researching people's opinions.

11. A boat washing ashore near the island that we have visited.

12. I would like to invite him to our party, he is outgoing.

13. Over the course of the next few years the changes that are proposed.

14. When you finish the assignment, take it to the printer, she will assist you.

15. My parents have Beach Boy albums in their record collection, I never play their records.

3-17. ALL 26

Each word below has one missing letter. On the line next to the misspelled word, write its correct spelling. If you fill in the correct letter in each word, you will use each of the alphabet's 26 letters—once. Use the letters below this paragraph to make sure you use each letter.

a b c d e f g h i j k l m n o p q r s t u v w x y z

sherif _____

backround _____

wayard _____

fleible _____

lmph _____

unecessary _____

monoply _____

mecanical _____

intenion _____

hiack _____

rabit _____

desel _____

immaulate _____

bookeeper _____

bazar _____

takative _____

landark _____

excessivly _____

acuire _____

aparel _____

conceie _____

mechant _____

omision _____

grizly _____

precios _____

wonerful _____

BECOMING MORE EFFICIENT

3-18. FOLLOWING YOUR TEACHER'S SUGGESTIONS

Your teacher reviews your writing progress and often suggests tips for improvement. Here are 15 sentences with "teacher suggestions" to make your writing even better. On the lines provided, follow the suggestions offered within the parentheses.

1. I can see you. (*add an adverb*) _____

2. This is the easiest way. (*add an infinitive phrase*) _____

3. The elephant was out of sorts. (*add a participle phrase*) _____

   _____

4. Take this package. (*add a prepositional phrase*) _____

   _____

5. We will read this information later. (*add a subordinate clause*) _____

   _____

6. Mr. Bucci is the new fire chief. (*add an appositive*) _____

   _____

7. Your method is helpful. (*add an adjective*) _____

8. Missy is the most talented skater. (*add an independent clause*) _____

   _____

9. The doctor thanked her patience for their patients. (*correct the misused words*)

   _____

10. This here wallet that was given to me on the occasion of my birthday is my method of carrying my cards used to identify and my cards used to charge items. (*eliminate the wordiness*)

   _____

11. The couple walked along the shore. (*use a more specific verb*) _____

   _____

12. A bathing suit and towel is all you need. (*use the correct number verb*) _____

   _____

13. If one can read, he can comprehend this text. (*use correct number agreement*)

   _____

14. Rotating in the clothes dryer, Grandpa could see the towels. (*correct the misplaced modifier*)

   _____

15. Us guys can help you restructure the garage. (*correct the pronoun problem*)

   _____

3-19. COMBINING SENTENCES

Combine each group of sentences on a separate piece of paper. Make sure the combination is logical and that you have followed the rules of correct punctuation.

1. Hugh is intelligent. Hugh is interesting. Hugh is kind.

2. The storm is approaching. The storm is named Hurricane Bonnie. The storm will hit somewhere in North Carolina.

3. The scissors were found on the desk. The scissors were used to cut Jamey's hair. Kate cut Jamey's hair. The scissors have white handles.

4. Joe called his editor. His editor's name is Marcia. Marcia works for Sundial Books. Marcia is a hardworking editor.

5. Leonardo DiCaprio was born on November 11, 1974. He is an only child. He was named after the Renaissance artist Leonardo Da Vinci.

6. Jocelyn plays varsity basketball on her high school team. Jocelyn is being recruited by many Division I Colleges. Jocelyn is an A student. Jocelyn wants to be a dentist.

7. Propene is an alkene. Propene has three carbon atoms. Propene has six hydrogen atoms.

8. The Marshall Plan is named after George C. Marshall. He was the U.S. Secretary of State. He proposed a way that the United States could strengthen Europe's economy after World War II. The Marshall Plan was passed by Congress in 1947.

9. Gertrude Stein was born in 1874. Her birthplace is Allegheny, Pennsylvania. She loved to read the plays of William Shakespeare. She wrote <u>The Autobiography of Alice B. Toklas</u> in 1933.

10. The substitute teacher assigned a composition. She said the composition would count as a test grade. The reason why she assigned the composition is because we were talking.

3-20. METHODS OF TRANSPORTATION

Each of 10 original sentences has been broken up into three parts. Each part has corresponding letters associated with it. Match the three parts of each original sentence by matching one part from Group A, one part from Group B, and one part from Group C. If you have matched the three parts of each original sentence correctly, the corresponding letters will spell out, in order from Group A to Group C, methods of transportation. Write the answers on the appropriate lines below.

Group A

1. The movie producer (**pl**)
2. The rebel leader (**tr**)
3. The state's courtroom (**tro**)
4. Many of the ships (**au**)
5. The suspended player (**sl**)
6. Several workers (**s**)
7. Do you think (**gon**)
8. After he completed the paint job, (**sur**)
9. Without a helmet (**ca**)
10. The benign tumor (**car**)

Group B

the cyclist (**n**)
asked their boss (**ka**)
specializes in films (**an**)
had to pass (**t**)
has promised (**ai**)

he washed the brushes (**fbo**)
was removed (**ria**)
that the new rules (**do**)
was packed (**ll**)
was not permitted (**e**)

Group C

is asking for trouble. (**oes**)
through the Panama Canal. (**os**)
to overthrow the government. (**ns**)
concerning race relations. (**es**)
by the skilled surgeon. (**ges**)

and stored the cans. (**ards**)
with photographers and reporters. (**eys**)
will be accepted by the students? (**las**)
to sit in the team's dugout. (**ds**)
for an extra hour's pay. (**tes**)

Sentences   **Transporation**

1. _____

2. _____

3. _____

4. _____

5. _____

6. _____

7. _____

8. _____

9. _____

10. _____

3-21. PLACING THE PARTICIPLES PROPERLY

Fifteen participles have been removed from their original sentences. Match the most appropriate participle from Column B with its original sentence in Column A by writing the participle's letter in the correct space. Each participle is used only once. The first one is done for you.

Column A

1. The steps __I__ are beautiful.

2. The pipe ____ was repaired yesterday.

3. The birds ____ were captured on film.

4. The coach ____ was not pleased by the players' efforts.

5. The sofa ____ was very comfortable.

6. The house ____ was featured in several magazines.

7. The book ____ was ordered by the librarian.

8. The tree ____ had been planted many years ago.

9. Her nails ____ were used as models by the store owner.

10. His teeth ____ drew the dentist's compliments.

11. The seashells ____ were a nice touch to the beautiful landscape.

12. The lacrosse stick ____ could not be repaired.

13. The workers ____ were sweating profusely.

14. The accompanist ____ was pleased to work with the gifted pianist.

15. The mechanic ____ had sore muscles.

Column B

A. damaged during the highly competitive game

B. covered with ivy

C. decorated by the talented designer

D. delicately manicured

E. digging the large hole

F. exhorting her players to try harder

G. flossed and brushed daily

H. flying over the shore

I. leading up to the Capitol

J. leaking in the basement

K. lining the walkway up to their summer home

L. purchased in the town's department store

M. rotating the cumbersome tires

N. turning the music pages

O. written by Judy Blume

3-22. A DIFFERENT KIND OF PARAGRAPH

Most of the work for this paragraph is already done. Yet, the most important part of the paragraph is up to you. Based on the sense of the existing paragraph, fill in the missing portions with your own words. Your teacher has the original paragraph to see how similar your paragraph is to the original.

Today was not the _____. First, my alarm clock

_____. Then, because our hot water was

_____, I was forced to take

_____. Breakfast was not much better since we had

_____. Just when I thought things could not get worse,

_____. Since my bus had already

_____, I took a _____. Eight

dollars later, I arrived at school _____. There Mr. Ambrose, our

social studies teacher, sprang _____. Only two students passed;

needless to say, _____. Later, Justin Holiday, my lab partner,

said Mrs. Loftin, our _____, would not accept our lab report

since it did not have the _____ heading. Luckily, the last period

arrived and we were given _____ by our French teacher,

Madame Roget, who said she had had such a bad day that

_____. Should I tell her about my day? I think not!

3-23. ORDER IN THE PARAGRAPH

In the spaces below each group of sentences, write the letters of the sentences in the order they should appear in the paragraph. Discuss your answers with your classmates.

Paragraph One

A. Looking for a new challenge, she became principal of the Moore Street Elementary School and has effected valuable change.

B. Mrs. Santana, our retiring principal, is an outstanding educator.

C. Though she will not be seen in our school's halls next September, this hard-working woman's influence and efforts will be present in our schools.

D. Mrs. Santana has been in education for thirty-two years.

E. There she implemented many programs that have served as models for other districts, even some in other states.

F. After teaching third grade for ten years, she moved into the position of Curriculum Director.

G. She has focused on making the school an educational community in which students and teachers want to come to school and interact with one another.

The paragraph's order is _____, _____, _____, _____, _____, _____, _____.

Paragraph Two

A. This region was probably called *never-never land* or *country* because those who visited there vowed "never, never" to return.

B. Originally, however, it was Australian slang for an isolated, sparsely settled region and was first applied to all of Australia and then to the remote Australian outback of western Queensland and Central Australia.

C. Today *never-never land* usually signifies an unreal, imaginary, or ideal condition or place, as in "the never-never land" of the movies.

D. Sir James Barrie first gave the meaning of an imaginary place to *Never Land* in his play *Peter Pan*, having Peter teach the Darling children to fly away to the wonderful realm of a child's imagination.

E. Today the British sometimes call installment plans "never-never plans," because one's ownership of the goods bought on such plans lies far in the distance in never-never land.

The paragraph's order is _____, _____, _____, _____, _____.

© 1999 by John Wiley & Sons, Inc.

Name _____ Date _____ Period _____

3-24. TEN INTO ONE (TWICE)

Combine the following sentences into one paragraph. You may add or delete words, but you must retain the original ideas. Write the paragraph on the lines below. Then, to show your versatility, use the same ten original sentences and write another paragraph. Check for complete sentences, proper punctuation, and logical combination of ideas. Good luck!

1. The couple walked along the shore.

2. The couple collected shells.

3. The couple held hands during the walk.

4. The couple talked about their jobs during the walk.

5. The seagulls lined up along the shore.

6. Boats were cruising out in the water.

7. An airplane pulling an advertisement flew above the couple.

8. The waves crashed on the shore.

9. Children built sand castles during the couple's walk.

10. Fishermen checked their lines.

First paragraph:

_____

_____

_____

_____

_____

Second paragraph:

_____

_____

_____

_____

_____

3-25. RESTORING ORDER

These 12 sentences are taken from two paragraphs each consisting of six sentences. In the appropriate spaces below the last sentence, write the letters of the six sentences that belong together in each paragraph. Circle the paragraph's topic sentence letter.

A. One's freshman year away at college is a valuable learning experience.

B. Since the work is not steady, she must find ways to earn a living.

C. Competition is stiff and, as a result, few performers, at least early in their careers, can rely solely on income from their acting.

D. Unfortunately, that, in itself, can be a valuable lesson.

E. Meeting the challenges of demanding courses is paramount.

F. The life of an aspiring actress is challenging.

G. In order to be successful, the student must learn to live with other people his own age.

H. Often, though she may be quite talented, the young lady may not have the look that the casting director is looking for.

I. When auditions are held, she needs to prepare herself for the role by studying the character and learning the character's lines.

J. If the student does not perform up to the college's academic or discipline requirements, he could be dismissed.

K. Coping with the disappointment that rejection brings truly tests the woman's mettle and may be enough for her to look in another direction.

L. He must also become virtually self-sufficient since he can no longer rely on his parents for certain things.

One paragraph ____ ____ ____ ____ ____ ____

The other paragraph ____ ____ ____ ____ ____ ____

Name _____ Date _____ Period _____

3-26. TRANSITIONAL WORDS AND PHRASES

Thirty transitional words and phrases are hidden in this word-find puzzle. They are placed backward, forward, diagonally, and vertically. Circle the words and phrases. Learn to use the transitions in your writing.

```
N T N G W L R M M E Y H F L K T G Z V C I W N G
U S O J E X S M P A C N M S I L T F N D N X B R
C N I B M C A K G S I N B D M K H B B E T T S R
O H T I W G N O L A L S O R F O E S U C H A S H
N Q I I G J O A G R T F T O E F R G C U E T E L
S K D B L H O A T E Q T U W O T E E S S P L J
E Z D Y E Q S M L S T B H R L W F K O B A M E H
Q B A L F C S P S U N S E E T P O A G V M N H Y
U T N N I O A Z M L W I C H S H R Q R P E F T K
E W I E X K R U V T K G R T P A E L F D W R R Z
N D Z D C C E E S T C W V O Z T M R N D A G E T
T D M D Q T Z W X E W H F N F C M E M D Y H V F
L Y G U L H Z V I A Z C Z I L C R L T O N F E R
Y Z F S N S Z N W S M Y M N P D C B H I R H N F
F W M K X S C M V M E P R F Y M R V S L M E E M
B Z M Q H M Y G H Y W D L R K X G M N C G E H R
T X G K N R G D I F F E R E N T F R O M K P W X
```

after	consequently	likewise	thus
again	different from	moreover	until
along with	for example	nevertheless	whenever
also	for instance	once	
as a result	furthermore	soon	
as soon as	in addition	such as	
at the same time	in other words	suddenly	
because	in the same way	then	
before	like	therefore	

3-27. MAKING THE DISTINCTION

The intelligent reader can tell the difference between what is a fact and what is an opinion. Thus, the astute writer should make the distinction between fact and opinion. If the topic is Boston, a factual sentence would be "Boston is the capital of Massachusetts." An opinion sentence is "Boston is one of the most picturesque cities in North America." Ten topics are listed below. For each topic write one factual sentence followed by one opinion sentence.

1. Cars _____

   Cars _____

2. Weekends _____

   Weekends _____

3. New Year's Eve _____

   New Year's Eve _____

4. Poetry _____

   Poetry _____

5. Computers _____

   Computers _____

6. Dentists _____

   Dentists _____

7. Compact discs _____

   Compact discs _____

8. Rain _____

   Rain _____

9. Exercise _____

   Exercise _____

10. Relatives _____

    Relatives _____

3-28. FACT VERSUS OPINION

Fourteen of the following sentences are facts, and six of the sentences are opinions. Write the letter **F** on the line next to the "fact sentences," and the letter **O** next to the "opinion sentences."

1. _____ Smoking contributes to lung cancer.

2. _____ Reading romance novels is thrilling for most people.

3. _____ Cuba is an island.

4. _____ Learning how to drive is stressful.

5. _____ Contact lenses are expensive.

6. _____ A paragraph's topic sentence should have a topic and an opinion.

7. _____ *The New York Times* is America's most interesting newspaper.

8. _____ Lisbon is Portugal's capital.

9. _____ The Democratic Party members are more caring than the Republican Party members.

10. _____ Former basketball player Michael Jordan is the world's best athlete.

11. _____ She is the world's most beautiful model.

12. _____ People are overly concerned with the problems of the rain forest.

13. _____ Laughter is the best medicine.

14. _____ England's Prince William is quite handsome.

15. _____ Earthquakes cause devastation.

16. _____ Harvard is America's most beloved college.

17. _____ Memorizing facts is beneficial for recalling information.

18. _____ Watching television programs is more educational than reading magazines.

19. _____ The voting age should be twenty-one.

20. _____ The government should keep confidential records on all of its citizens.

3-29. DISTINGUISHING FACT FROM OPINION

Six topics are given to you. For each topic write the topic's definition on the first line and then write one opinion (thesis statement) on the second line. Discuss your answers with your classmates. An example is done for you.

Topic: Word-find puzzles
Definition: A word-find puzzle is a puzzle in which the letters of the words are placed diagonally, up and down, left to right, or right to left.
Opinion: Word-find puzzles are easy to solve.

1. **Topic:** VCR

   Definition: _____

   Opinion: _____

2. **Topic:** Classroom group projects

   Definition: _____

   Opinion: _____

3. **Topic:** Monster movies

   Definition: _____

   Opinion: _____

4. **Topic:** Subways

   Definition: _____

   Opinion: _____

5. **Topic:** The game called Monopoly®

   Definition: _____

   Opinion: _____

6. **Topic:** Middle school

   Definition: _____

   Opinion: _____

3-30. THE FACTS AND OPINIONS OF POETRY

On the line before each of these 15 lines of poetry, write whether the line is a FACT or an OPINION. If you feel that a line can be interpreted as both a fact and an opinion, write BOTH. Be ready to defend your answers. The poet and the name of the poem follow the poetic line.

1. _____ I'm a riddle in nine syllables. —Sylvia Plath, "Metaphors"

2. _____ Sundays my father got up early. —Robert Hayden, "Those Winter Sundays"

3. _____ He clasps the crag with crooked hands. —Alfred, Lord Tennyson, "The Eagle"

4. _____ The miller's wife had waited long. —Edward Arlington Robinson, "The Mill"

5. _____ The sea is calm tonight. —Matthew Arnold, "Dover Beach"

6. _____ Heavy is my heart. —Mary Coleridge, "Slowly"

7. _____ O my love is like a red, red rose. —Robert Burns, "A Red, Red Rose"

8. _____ There is no frigate like a book. —Emily Dickinson, "There Is No Frigate . . ."

9. _____ Nature the gentlest one there is. —Emily Dickinson, "Nature the Gentlest Mother"

10. _____ She should have died hereafter. —Shakespeare, *Macbeth*

11. _____ The price seemed reasonable. —Wole Soyinka, "Telephone Conversation"

12. _____ There's nothing mysterious about the skull. — Janet Burroway, "The Scientist"

13. _____ Nothing is plumb, level, or square. —Alan Dugan, "Love Song: I and Thou"

14. _____ Round the cape of a sudden came the sea. —Robert Browning, "Parting at Morning"

15. _____ This is the field where the battle did not happen. —William Stafford, "At the Un-National Monument Along the Canadian Border"

SECTION THREE

GENERATING IDEAS

3-31. DEVELOPING TOPIC SENTENCES

The topic sentence states the paragraph's main idea and indicates the paragraph's purpose. It is generally, though not always, found at or near the paragraph's beginning. Sometimes the topic sentence is implied rather than stated. Often facts, examples, incidents, and arguments help to develop the topic sentence's statement. In the space provided, use one of the developmental methods (facts, examples, incidents, or arguments) to show how you would develop each topic sentence. Try to use each method at least once. Your answers do not have to be in complete sentences. Be as specific as possible.

1. Smoking can be hazardous to your health.

_____

_____

_____

_____

2. Hard work generally pays off.

_____

_____

_____

_____

3. A college education can be rewarding in many ways.

_____

_____

_____

_____

4. A teenager's life is not as easy as some may think it is.

_____

_____

_____

_____

3-32. WORKING WITH TOPIC SENTENCES

A topic sentence needs a subject and an attitude, impression, or opinion about the subject. In the topic sentence, "The English language is one of the most difficult languages to learn," the topic is the English language and the attitude is that it is "one of the most difficult languages to learn." For each topic sentence below, circle the topic and underline the attitude.

1. Jogging helps people keep fit.

2. Richard is our most challenging opponent.

3. Cultural biases are detrimental to a society's well-being.

4. Researching one's family history is an eye-opening experience.

5. E-mail is more exciting than postal mail.

6. Taxpayers are anxious about their tax returns.

7. Atticus Finch, the father in Harper Lee's *To Kill a Mockingbird,* is one of literature's most memorable characters.

8. A day at the beach is the most exhilarating experience for the Morton family.

9. The columnist's article is a brilliant piece of journalism.

10. The lion is the most interesting animal to study.

11. Discipline is a necessity for success in life.

12. The Pine Barrens, the island's pristine section, should not be commercially developed.

13. Alfred Hitchcock was one of the most talented movie directors.

14. Insignificant school rules are troublesome.

15. Cancer detection should remain one of the country's medical priorities.

Name _____ Date _____ Period _____

3-33. TOPIC SENTENCE REVIEW

The following topic sentences need to be completed. On the line within each sentence, complete the topic sentence. Then select four of your topic sentences and, on the reverse side of this paper, write three examples to support your opinion. Share your answers with your classmates.

1. People should not _____.

2. The best way to reconcile differences is _____.

3. _____ is the best season of the year.

4. _____ is the most effective form of exercise.

5. _____ is the world's most glamorous job.

6. Vegetarians are _____.

7. High school is _____.

8. No teen should _____.

9. Today's music _____.

10. Budgeting one's money _____.

11. An important lesson for me was _____.

12. Owning your own business _____.

13. One of my country's problems is _____.

14. A chore I dislike is _____.

15. The death penalty is _____.

3-34. THE THESIS STATEMENT

A thesis statement consists of a topic and an opinion that you will attempt to prove within your essay. Thus, if the topic is *downhill skiing*, an effective thesis statement is "Downhill skiing is one of the most challenging winter activities." Following this thesis statement, you would set out to prove your contention with supportive examples concerning downhill skiing. Remember that a thesis statement is *not* a fact. It is a provable opinion that could very possibly be argued by an opposing opinion about that topic. One could argue that downhill skiing is *not* one of the most challenging winter activities.

Directions: For any ten of the following topics, construct a thesis statement. Write this sentence on the line following the topic.

1. Pollution: _____

2. Law enforcement personnel: _____

3. The Summer Olympics: _____

4. Prejudice: _____

5. Reincarnation: _____

6. Jails: _____

7. Exercise: _____

8. After-school sports: _____

9. Reading: _____

10. Voting: _____

11. Vacations: _____

12. The elderly: _____

13. Newspapers: _____

14. Amusement parks: _____

15. Relatives: _____

3-35. SUPPORTING YOUR THESIS STATEMENT

The five quotes below are also good thesis statements. For each quote, write three specific examples that support the thesis. Then select your strongest thesis statement along with its supporting evidence, and write a composition using that thesis statement as the first sentence of the composition. Entitle your composition. An example of a thesis statement and its support is done for you.

"Easy reading is hard writing."

1. Select an appropriate purpose and an interesting topic.
2. Utilizing effective sentence structure and sentence variety.
3. Choosing the most appropriate word to suit the purpose.

Ralph Waldo Emerson: "Nothing is accomplished without enthusiasm."

_____

_____

_____

German proverb: "Patience is a bitter plant, but it has sweet fruit."

_____

_____

_____

Alexander Pope: "Fools rush in where angels fear to tread."

_____

_____

_____

Joseph Joubert: "Children need models rather than critics."

_____

_____

_____

Yiddish proverb: "He that lies on the ground cannot fail."

_____

_____

_____

Name _____ Date _____ Period _____

3-36. GIVING GOOD REASONS

Four opinionated sentences are below. Using the format of the example, offer substantive reasons to support your position. Choose at least four strong, supporting reasons to defend yourself. Write your answers on a separate piece of paper. Then choose two of your four answers and write a paragraph for each. Start with the topic sentence and then include the supportive reasons within the paragraph. An example paragraph is offered to you.

Nancy should be selected for the school's soccer team.

1. She is a skilled player.

2. She is in good physical condition and can withstand the strenuous demands of the game.

3. Her attitude is exemplary. She works hard and will accept a position as a starter or a substitute maturely.

4. She is a team player. Her former teammates compliment her on her unselfish attitude.

5. She has playing experience and knows the game well.

Nancy, a skilled soccer player, should be selected for the school's team. She is in good physical condition and can withstand the strenuous demands of the game. Having an exemplary attitude, Nancy works hard and will accept a position as either a starter or a substitute. Her former teammates compliment Nancy, a team player, on her unselfish attitude. She has playing experience and knows the game of soccer well.

1. The driving age will be pushed back by two years.

2. The school year will be extended to 240 days instead of the current 180 days.

3. Your parents refuse to allow you to go away with your friend's family for a week this summer to their summer house three hundred miles away.

4. Your parents refuse to allow you to tune into a show they feel you are not old enough to watch.

3-37. EXPRESSING YOURSELF

Here is your chance to write a paragraph showing how you are *for* or *against* a statement. For each of these five issues, take a stand and give specific examples to defend your position. State your position in the first line and then include at least four sentences of supportive evidence for your position.

1. Some song lyrics promote violence.

_____
_____
_____
_____
_____

2. The minimum wage should be increased.

_____
_____
_____
_____
_____

3. The school day should be extended another two hours.

_____
_____
_____
_____
_____

4. Teens do not read enough.

_____
_____
_____
_____
_____

5. The death penalty is wrong.

_____
_____
_____
_____
_____

3-38. SUPPORTING YOUR OPINIONS

For each of the following thesis statements, write three strong supporting pieces of evidence. You do not have to write these pieces of evidence in complete sentences. An example is done for you. Write your answers on a separate piece of paper.

> **Thesis statement:** A college education contributes to one's financial success in the business world. **Evidence:**
>
> (A) Statistics prove that college-educated workers generally make more money than noncollege-educated workers over their lifetimes.
>
> (B) Thinking skills learned in college are used to solve problems and make greater financial profits in the business world.
>
> (C) Businesses generally hire college-educated men and women to fill the higher-paying jobs within the company.

1. Picnics are fun.

2. Football is a dangerous sport.

3. Scrapbooks make great gifts.

4. Some school rules are unnecessary.

5. Delivering a speech is nerve-wracking.

6. Drawing a portrait is painstaking work.

7. Classroom discussions are an effective learning tool.

8. Smoking is dangerous to one's health.

9. It is what is inside a person that really counts.

10. Actions speak louder than words.

3-39. SUPPORTING YOUR CHOICE

Each Friday a national television network selects its "Person of the Week." Each year *Time* magazine selects its "Person of the Year." These choices are not made quickly. Instead, they are reached after careful deliberation. Strong reasons to support the committee's choice are offered. If weak reasons are offered, the choice does not stand a chance. The same holds true with your writing. When you are writing to persuade, powerful supportive evidence must be presented.

Directions: First circle one of the awards below. Then select your choice for this award. Offer four reasons why your choice should be given this award. After each reason, illustrate that evidence. Thus, if the category is "My Favorite Sport," one of your reasons why swimming is your favorite sport could be that "swimming is a great cardiovascular activity." An example could be "swimming burns more calories than almost any other activity."

The categories are **Movie of the Year; Teacher of the Year; Music Video of the Year; Song of the Year; World's Greatest Athlete; The Greatest Invention;** or (fill in your own category here).

_____.

My candidate for this award is _____.

My first reason: _____.

An example of this is _____.

My second reason: _____.

An example of this is _____.

My third reason: _____.

An example of this is _____.

My fourth reason: _____.

An example of this is _____.

3-40. SUPPORTING YOURSELF ON SCHOOL ISSUES

Your community's school board has come up with some interesting proposals for the next school year. Select any five of the following ten proposals and, for each proposal, list at least three reasons why you are *for* or *against* the planned change. Write your answers on a separate sheet of paper. Your reasons do not have to be in complete sentences. Share your responses with your classmates.

(A) School yearbooks will be discontinued.

(B) Each student must perform thirty hours of community service this year.

(C) School lunch programs will double in price.

(D) All students will read three novels this summer.

(E) Detention will be held on Saturday mornings.

(F) Once a year a parent must spend the entire school day with his or her child.

(G) Bus service will be eliminated due to budget cuts.

(H) Students will vote on whether a teacher is rehired for the next academic year.

(I) No new computers will be purchased for the next three years.

(J) Each student must pay an annual fee of two hundred dollars to participate in extracurricular activities.

3-41. TAKING A STAND ON LITERATURE

Two quotations by well-known authors appear below. Choose one of the two quotations. Then, using two different works of literature, write two separate paragraphs, one for each literary work, arguing your position (*for* or *against*) regarding this quotation. Each paragraph should include a topic sentence and one or more pieces of strong, supporting evidence. Include the name of the literary work and remember that a novel's title is underlined. Write the two paragraphs on the lines provided for you. (Use the back of this sheet if you need more space.)

Quote # 1: The only good books that influence us are those for which we are ready, and which have gone a little farther down our particular path than we have yet gone ourselves. —*E. M. Forster*

Quote # 2: There is no such thing as a moral or immoral book. Books are well written or badly written. That is all.   —*Oscar Wilde*

First literary work:

_____

_____

_____

_____

_____

_____

_____

_____

Second literary work:

_____

_____

_____

_____

_____

_____

_____

_____

3-42. SELECT, STATE, AND NARROW

First, select one of the following topics. Then write a thesis statement for that topic. Next, narrow the topic by writing at least three specific supporting examples. Use another sheet of paper to record your answers. An example is given to you.

> **Bumper stickers:** Bumper stickers express the car owner's opinions. (a) political—"McPhee is the candidate for me." (b) humorous—"My other car is a piece of junk, too!" (c) achievement—"My child is on the Monroe Street School Honor Roll."

1. homework

2. bathing suits

3. fitness programs

4. television talk shows

5. school final exams

6. gangs

7. credit cards

8. authority

9. loneliness

10. war

3-43. LISTING YOUR IDEAS

Listing is an effective writer's tool to gather ideas and show their relationship to one another. Start with a nucleus word and then list words related to that nucleus word. Record all of your thoughts.

Five topics that can be used as nucleus words are below. On the lines provided, list ideas related to the nucleus word. List as many ideas as possible since you might be asked to focus this topic better in the near future. Think of what major categories can be part of this topic. An example of a nucleus word's related words is done for you.

> **VEHICLES** land, cars, bicycles, sleds, go-carts, motorcycles, buses, water, ships, boats, canoes, kayaks, barges, ocean liners, airplanes, jets, helicopters, rockets

1. MUSIC

_____

_____

_____

2. PHYSICAL FITNESS

_____

_____

_____

3. CLOTHING

_____

_____

_____

4. PARENTS

_____

_____

_____

5. MEDIA

_____

_____

_____

3-44. THINKING ABOUT TOPICS

Fifteen topics are listed below. For any ten of these topics, list four sub-topics that you could use if asked to write an essay on this topic. Thus, if the topic is Divorce, sub-topics could include the causes of divorce, the effects of divorce on the couple, the effects of divorce on the couple's children, and the financial costs of a divorce. On a separate sheet of paper, write the four sub-topics for each of your ten choices. Share your answers with your classmates.

1. Physical Exercise

2. Grandma (or Grandpa)

3. War

4. A Model Zoo

5. Community Sports (or Arts) Programs

6. Children's Television

7. Teen Magazines

8. Dating

9. Comic Strips

10. Bumper Stickers

11. Soap Operas

12. Making Friends

13. High School Life

14. Professional Athletes

15. Malls

3-45. DEVELOPING THE TOPIC

If you had to develop each of the following four topics, which approaches could you use? These possible approaches include analyzing, classifying, arguing, comparing, contrasting, evaluating, describing, informing, and narrating. On the appropriate lines, list four approaches you could take to write an essay on that given topic. An example is done for you.

> **Example:** The French Government and the Kenyan Government—Two Different Systems
>
> a. analyze the components of each
>
> b. argue which is more (or less) effective
>
> c. classify each according to its philosophy
>
> d. compare and contrast the two systems

1. Today's Musical Lyrics

   _____

   _____

   _____

   _____

2. Technology's Effects on Your Life vs. Life at the Turn of the 19th Century

   _____

   _____

   _____

   _____

3. A Typical Teen's Life Today

   _____

   _____

   _____

   _____

4. The State of Today's Education

   _____

   _____

   _____

   _____

3-46. A TOPIC'S DEVELOPMENT

When your teacher assigns a writing assignment and asks you to choose your approach to writing the assignment, there are several methods you can use. These methods are explained below. For each of the 15 topic assignments, identify the method you would use to write the composition by writing the method's letter on the appropriate line. If you feel a topic can be approached in more than one way, list the other method(s). In all cases, be ready to defend your answers.

Methods

(A) **Cause and effect:** What caused something to happen? What consequences did it have?

(B) **Classification:** Classifying a number of people, things, concepts, and the like into groups based on their similarities and differences.

(C) **Comparison—contrast:** How are two people, places, things, ideas, and the like similar and different?

(D) **Definition:** Establish the essential meaning and cite the general class and a distinction. "A marathon is a foot race covering 26.2 miles" is an example of definition.

(E) **Description:** To describe a person, place, thing, or idea using sensory images.

(F) **Division or analysis:** Show the components of a structure. This usually involves a single subject, such as the French Government.

(G) **Illustration or Example:** An example represents a general group or an abstract quality.

(H) **Narration:** Tell a story by answering the questions Who? Where? When? What?

(I) **Process:** Lists and explains the steps of a process.

Topics

1. _____ Apples

2. _____ Cooking a Turkey Dinner

3. _____ The Murder of Abraham Lincoln

4. _____ Does Stress Improve an Athlete's Performance?

5. _____ Who Is the Better Actress—Meryl Streep or Glenn Close?

6. _____ What Was Henry Ford's Model T?

7. _____ Is Sherlock Holmes the Typical Fictional Detective?

8. _____ Exercise Can Change Your Life

9. _____ My English Teacher

10. _____ The Day My Family Moved

11. _____ How to Get into a Good College

12. _____ All Restaurants Are Not the Same

13. _____ Today's Political Leaders

14. _____ The Dangers of the Internet on Children

15. _____ Honor

SECTION FOUR

ZEROING IN

3-47. PARAPHRASING

To paraphrase is to restate the meaning of someone else's idea in your own words. A paraphrase of the proverb "An apple a day keeps the doctor away" is " Eat healthy foods." Paraphrase each of the following ten quotations. Write your paraphrase on the line provided for you. The quotation's author appears after the quotation.

1. The only gift is a portion of thyself. —*Ralph Waldo Emerson*

   _____

2. A good cook is a slow poisoner, if you are not temperate. —*Voltaire*

   _____

3. The truth is always the strongest argument. —*Sophocles*

   _____

4. Time heals what reason can't. —*Seneca*

   _____

5. All lay load on the willing horse. —*English proverb*

   _____

6. Friendship is like money, easier made than kept. —*Samuel Johnson*

   _____

7. One falsehood spoils a thousand truths. —*Ashanti proverb*

   _____

8. Be content with your lot; you cannot be first in everything. —*Aesop*

   _____

9. Laws are silent in time of war. —*Cicero*

   _____

10. Wedlock, a padlock. —*English proverb*

   _____

3-48. REWORDING MEMORABLE WORDS

A good writer makes words work. This writer often creates a sentence and then, for one or another reason, rearranges it, inserting and deleting words when necessary. This activity asks you to use an original sentence and then paraphrase it. Essentially, say what the original sentence says, but use other words. On the line below each quotation, write that quotation in other words. An example is given to you. The quotation's author follows the quotation.

> Example: It is easy to be brave from a safe distance. (Aesop)
> <u>True bravery demands action.</u>

1. Man is not the creature of circumstances. Circumstances are the creatures of men.
   —*Benjamin Disraeli*

   _____

2. Never buy what you do not want because it is cheap; it will be dear [costly] to you.
   —*Thomas Jefferson*

   _____

3. Democracy is good. I say this because other systems are worse.   —*Jawaharlal Nehru*

   _____

4. Happiness depends upon ourselves.   —*Aristotle*

   _____

5. Poverty is no disgrace, but no honor either.   —*Yiddish proverb*

   _____

6. Reputation is an idle and most false imposition; oft got without merit and lost without deserving.   —*Shakespeare*

   _____

7. I can resist everything except temptation.   —*Oscar Wilde*

   _____

8. The heaviest baggage for a traveler is an empty purse.   —*English proverb*

   _____

9. The test of the vocation is the love of the drudgery it involves.   —*Logan Pearsall*

   _____

10. Riches do not consist in the possession of treasures, but in the use made of them.
    —*Napolean I*

    _____

11. No tears in the writer, no tears in the reader.   —*Robert Frost*

    _____

12. Friendship often ends in love; but love in friendship—never.   —*Charles Caleb Colton*

    _____

3-49. SHOW US HOW THEY FEEL

Twelve different people are listed below with an emotion, trait, or state of being next to their name. For each person write an illustrative sentence that effectively demonstrates that person's emotion, trait, or state of being. For example, if the name *George* has the word *anticipation* next to it, an illustrative sentence could read, "George was very eager to hear his sister's news." Here you have effectively demonstrated a mood of anticipation on George's part. Do the same for these twelve people. Do not include the original word or any form of it in your illustrative sentence.

1. Kaneesha (fright) _____

_____

2. Paula (anger) _____

_____

3. Joyce (curiosity) _____

_____

4. Kim-Li (nervousness) _____

_____

5. Dennis (indifference) _____

_____

6. Mike (boredom) _____

_____

7. Brian (dread) _____

_____

8. Madeline (silliness) _____

_____

9. Jose (amusement) _____

_____

10. Lorraine (longing) _____

_____

11. Carol (understanding) _____

_____

12. Roberto (doubt) _____

_____

3-50. LET'S GET EMOTIONAL

Twelve emotions, qualities, or states of being are listed below. For each, write an illustrative sentence that effectively exhibits that emotion, quality, or state of being. Thus, if the sentence reads, "Scott could hardly sit still as he waited to hear the news of his medical tests," the mood exemplified could be nervousness or anxiety or uneasiness. Do not use the word or any form of it in your sentence. Dictionary help is advisable. Then check to see how effective your sentences are by asking your classmates to identify the word you have illustrated after you have read your sentences to them.

1. joy _____
   _____

2. confusion _____
   _____

3. pressure _____
   _____

4. contentment _____
   _____

5. determination _____
   _____

6. prejudice _____
   _____

7. courage _____
   _____

8. honor _____
   _____

9. honesty _____
   _____

10. love _____
    _____

11. loneliness _____
    _____

12. kindness _____
    _____

3-51. SHOWING THE CONTRASTS

A good writer brainstorms an idea and lists the ideas that come to mind. From there, the writer focuses first on concepts and then on specifics. With more hard work, the writer completes the process of composition.

Four contrasting situations are found below. In the spaces provided, write whatever comes to mind after you have read and thought about the situation. Show how the contrasting situations differ. Your answers should be notes, not complete sentences. Share your responses with your classmates.

1. The beach on a hot summer day. _____

_____

_____

The same beach on a frigid winter day. _____

_____

_____

2. You and your best friend are told by the coach that you have both made the school team.

_____

_____

The coach tells you that you have made the team, but your best friend has not.

_____

_____

3. Your school's cafeteria in the middle of the first lunch period on the opening day of school

_____

_____

Your school's cafeteria immediately after the last lunch period that same day.

_____

_____

4. Your mom tells you that your family is moving three hundred miles away.

_____

_____

Your mom tells you that your family is not moving three hundred miles away as planned.

_____

_____

3-52. WORKING WITH QUOTATIONS

Writers will sometimes use quotations of well-known people to emphasize important concepts. Skillfully knowing when and how to use these quotations is beneficial to both the writer and the reader.

Ten topics are listed below. Ten quotations along with their authors follow. Match the quotation with its appropriate topic. Write the correct topic in the space next to the number. Each topic is used only once.

bribery	consistency	existence	intelligence	reputation
competition	excess	heredity	privacy	tradition

1. _____ We spend our lives talking about this mystery: our life.
—*Jules Renard*

2. _____ The archer that shoots over, misses as much as he that falls short. —*Montaigne*

3. _____ Deep in the cavern of the infant's breast/The father's nature lurks, and lives anew. —*Horace*

4. _____ Life is for one generation; a good name is forever.
—*Japanese proverb*

5. _____ He may well win the race that runs by himself.
—*Benjamin Franklin*

6. _____ A hedge between keeps friendship green. —*German proverb*

7. _____ To the dull mind all nature is leaden. To the illuminated mind the whole world burns and sparkles with light.
—*Ralph Waldo Emerson*

8. _____ The dead govern the living. —*Auguste Comte*

9. _____ It is not best to swap horses while crossing the river.
—*Abraham Lincoln*

10. _____ A friend that you buy with presents will be bought from you.
—*Thomas Fuller*

3-53. WHAT IS THE DIFFERENCE?

Show you know the difference between the two words in each pair by writing an illustrative sentence that features the first word and then another illustrative sentence that features the second word. Write each sentence on its appropriate line. The first pair is done for you.

1. **chuckle vs. guffaw**
   The woman chuckled when she thought about the amusing story.

   The coarse man guffawed after he heard the caustic remark.

2. **task vs. assignment**
   _____

   _____

3. **short vs. dwarfish**
   _____

   _____

4. **aptitude vs. gift**
   _____

   _____

5. **funny vs. hilarious**
   _____

   _____

6. **friend vs. acquaintance**
   _____

   _____

7. **mansion vs. hut**
   _____

   _____

8. **ponder vs. consider**
   _____

   _____

9. **alter vs. convert**
   _____

   _____

10. **difficult vs. impossible**
   _____

   _____

3-54. ILLUSTRATIVE SENTENCES

An illustrative sentence clearly displays the word you are asked to exemplify. "The players jumped high in the air when their teammate scored the winning goal" is an illustrative sentence showing the word *happiness*. Construct an illustrative sentence for each word below. Do not use the word or any form of the word in your illustrative sentence.

1. civil: _____

_____

2. meditate: _____

_____

3. toxic: _____

_____

4. ludicrous: _____

_____

5. immature: _____

_____

6. arsenal: _____

_____

7. eloquent: _____

_____

8. antagonize: _____

_____

9. emulate: _____

_____

10. observant: _____

_____

11. intriguing: _____

_____

12. agile: _____

_____

13. jovial: _____

_____

14. persevere: _____

_____

15. sophisticated: _____

_____

3-55. USING THE CORRECT WORD

A good writer uses the best word, the most exact word, to fit the situation. This crossword puzzle features words that are much the same, but different in one way or another. Write your answers to these clues in the appropriate spaces. Good luck!

ACROSS

4. to laugh slowly in a low tone
6. a natural tendency or ability
8. an intimate associate
9. to modify; to make different in detail, but not in substance
12. a task that one has been given by another
14. stunted as a result of deformity
15. low in height; not tall
16. a large and stately residence
18. boisterous and gay; very funny; noisily merry

DOWN

1. one who knows you, but not intimately
2. to laugh in a coarse burst of laughter
3. a cabin of the plainest kind
5. an inland body of water larger than a pond
7. a body of water smaller than a lake
8. amusing; humorous
10. a piece of work involving labor or difficulty
11. to change from one form or use to another
13. not capable of being done
14. hard; requiring extra thought or effort
17. notably superior talent

3-56. A SENSATIONAL ASSIGNMENT

This activity will allow you to make good use of your sentences. For each of the following places or events, give an example of each sense's perception. Show what you hear, see, smell, touch, and taste at that place or event. Then, for any two of these, write a paragraph including a topic sentence and the results of your five senses. Write the paragraphs on a separate piece of paper.

1. **An amusement park**

hearing: _____

sight: _____

smell: _____

touch: _____

taste: _____

2. **Your school's cafeteria**

hearing: _____

sight: _____

smell: _____

touch: _____

taste: _____

3. **A family gathering**

hearing: _____

sight: _____

smell: _____

touch: _____

taste: _____

4. **A school dance**

hearing: _____

sight: _____

smell: _____

touch: _____

taste: _____

5. **A meal at a local fast-food restaurant**

hearing: _____

sight: _____

smell: _____

touch: _____

taste: _____

3-57. NOTING AN AUTHOR'S OPINION

As a writer, you will utilize verbs that clearly express your approach toward a topic. The following 20 verbs do just that. Four approaches to a topic are listed below. Read the explanation of each approach. Then, next to each of the 20 words, write the approach's corresponding letter. Discuss your answers with your classmates.

(A) *Neutral:* The author does not indicate a liking or a distaste for the topic.

(B) *Argument:* The author displays an opinion that can be *for* or *against* the topic.

(C) *Negativity:* The author dislikes the topic.

(D) *Implication:* The author suggests something.

1. ____ defends

2. ____ analyzes

3. ____ predicts

4. ____ explains

5. ____ proposes

6. ____ complains

7. ____ derides

8. ____ comments

9. ____ insists

10. ____ belittles

11. ____ illustrates

12. ____ condemns

13. ____ observes

14. ____ describes

15. ____ claims

16. ____ contends

17. ____ deplores

18. ____ speculates

19. ____ writes

20. ____ sees

3-58. TIME OUT FOR SOME FUN WITH OXYMORONS

An oxymoron is a figure of speech in which contradictory terms are combined. "Thunderous silence" is an oxymoron. The first words of 22 oxymorons are in Column A. Match them with their second words by writing the appropriate two-letter answer from Column B on the line in Column A. The first one is done for you. If your answers are correct, they will spell out (in order) a quotation and the quotation's source. Write the quotation and its source at the bottom of this page.

Column A	Column B
1. <u>he</u> act	(AN) crowd
2. _____ alone	(AR) ugly
3. _____ clearly	(EA) difference
4. _____ definite	(ES) missing
5. _____ diet	(EW) dead
6. _____ found	(GE) imitation
7. _____ genuine	(HE) naturally
8. _____ hot water	(HP) bet
9. _____ jumbo	(ID) ice cream
10. _____ living	(IS) rock
11. _____ passive	(IV) maybe
12. _____ peace	(OD) misunderstood
13. _____ plastic	(OR) aggression
14. _____ pretty	(RB) vacation
15. _____ same	(RO) sorrow
16. _____ silent	(SH) glasses
17. _____ small	(SP) scream
18. _____ soft	(ST) force
19. _____ sure	(TH) shrimp
20. _____ sweet	(TS) heater
21. _____ tight	(VE) slacks
22. _____ working	(WH) together

Quotation: _____

Source: _____

3-59. TRACING THE SOURCE

Match each word or expression in Column A with its source in Column B by placing the correct two-letter answer in the appropriate space. If your answers are correct, you will spell out five synonyms for the word *source*. Write those five synonyms at the bottom of the page.

Column A

1. _____ Achilles Heel
2. _____ atlas
3. _____ boycott
4. _____ Braille
5. _____ Herculean
6. _____ Judas
7. _____ malapropism
8. _____ mentor
9. _____ Midas touch
10. _____ Pollyanna
11. _____ Reaganomics
12. _____ sandwich
13. _____ silhouette
14. _____ stygian
15. _____ tantalize

Column B

AR. a Titan who supported the world on his shoulders

BR. a mythological river

EM. a French controller general

EN. one blinded by an awl at three years old

ES. mythical Greek who performed twelve labors

IG. a wise counselor in mythology

IN. a greedy mythological king

IS. Christ's betrayer

NG. slices of meat and a card game

OR. a word blunderer in Sheridan's play *The Rivals*

RI. American president

SP. female character who looked for the bright side

ST. a Trojan War warrior

TG. a stubborn British soldier

YO. mythological king who revealed the secrets of the gods to humans

Five synonyms for *source:* _____

_____

3-60. IDIOMS

In formal writing, writers generally avoid using idioms, those expressions that cannot be understood literally. So expressions such as "chip off the old block," "in mint condition," and "eat someone out of house and home" should be avoided. On the line next to each idiom, write the idiom's meaning. Then, in your future writings, instead of using idioms, use more exact ways to say the same thing.

1. to lend an ear _____

2. dead to the world _____

3. everything but the kitchen sink _____

4. to build castles in the air _____

5. to make a long story short _____

6. to get down to brass tacks _____

7. to put the cart before the horse _____

8. take the bull by the horns _____

9. six of one and a half dozen of the other _____

10. come up in the world _____

11. to make the grade _____

12. to turn the other cheek _____

13. to bite one's tongue _____

14. to work one's fingers to the bones _____

15. lead someone down the wrong path _____

16. not born yesterday _____

17. at a snail's pace _____

18. all thumbs _____

19. birds of a feather _____

20. pick up the tab _____

DEVELOPING SKILLS

3-61. SETTING DOWN THE TERMS

On the appropriate lines, define each of these terms associated with essay writing. Be as specific as possible. Compare your answers with those of your classmates.

1. What is meant by the writer's audience?

   _____

   _____

2. What is meant by the essay's content?

   _____

   _____

3. What are the different forms of writing?

   _____

   _____

4. What are some purposes of writing?

   _____

   _____

5. Define the term *clarity* regarding writing.

   _____

   _____

6. What is diction?

   _____

   _____

7. What is a fragment?

   _____

   _____

8. What is a run-on?

   _____

   _____

9. What is the writer's voice?

   _____

   _____

10. What is meant by the writer's personal touch?

   _____

   _____

3-62. SOME FOOD FOR THOUGHT REGARDING THE PARAGRAPH

Here are ten questions dealing with paragraphs. Write the correct answers in the appropriate spaces. Use the back of this sheet if necessary.

1. The topic sentence is generally positioned at the _____ of the paragraph.

2. The necessary components of the topic sentence include a _____ and an _____.

3. A thesis statement can either be <u>stated</u> or <u>implied</u>. Explain each of the underlined words.

4. A topic sentence does not always appear as a paragraph's first sentence. Why?

   _____

   _____

5. What is the purpose of supporting sentences?

   _____

6. Explain how a fact and an opinion are different.

   _____

7. Place the letter **F** after a group of words that is a fact. Place an **O** after a group of words that is an opinion.

   A. Ben Franklin was an American political figure. _____

   B. Her argument regarding presidential power is profound. _____

   C. Adults are not always aware of the stress that teens experience. _____

   D. Swimming is both a boring and repetitive activity. _____

   E. A fragment is part of a sentence. _____

8. Does the word <u>thesis</u> more closely describe a fact or an opinion? Why?

9. Construct a topic sentence for the following paragraph:

   The high school band played throughout the town's two-hour Memorial Day parade. Boy Scouts and Girl Scouts marched with their troop leaders. Town officials led the parade. The fire trucks were the last vehicles. Twirlers performed their routines.

10. Insert a topic sentence at the *end* of this paragraph:

    New York City has many restaurants featuring foods from many different countries. Central Park provides exercise opportunity and relaxation. Tall buildings line many of New York City's streets. Department stores, specialty stores, bookstores, movies, museums, theaters, and sports arenas are also found there.

3-63. DESCRIBING PEOPLE, PLACES, AND THINGS

Select a name for each item below. Then, for each letter in that item, write a characteristic adjective that accurately describes the person, place, or thing. (An example appears below.) Now select your favorite answer and, on a separate piece of paper, write a paragraph for at least four of those adjectives. Your goal in each paragraph is to effectively illustrate that characteristic.

An animal: <u>tiger</u> tough, instinctive, gruff, energetic, renowned

A relative: _____

A friend: _____

A pet: _____

A literary character: _____

A teacher: _____

A coach: _____

A food: _____

A television character: _____

A movie: _____

A newspaper: _____

A country: _____

A song's title: _____

A vacation spot: _____

Your town: _____

3-64. WRITING A REPORT

In your academic classes, you are often asked to takes notes during an oral presentation, a film, or a reading. Then you are asked to combine the notes into a report.

Directions: Here are eighteen facts about William Shakespeare. On a separate piece of paper, combine these 18 facts into a logical, well-written composition. Include all the facts, vary the types of sentences, use paragraphing, and place the sentences in a logical order.

— was born in Stratford-Upon-Avon in 1564

— married Anne Hathaway in 1582

— had a patron, the Earl of Southampton

— wrote 154 sonnets

— purchased a large house, New Place, in Stratford in 1597

— types of plays included histories, comedies, and tragedies

— died on his birthday, April 23, in 1616 at the age of 52

— memorable tragic characters include Romeo, Juliet, Macbeth, Hamlet, and Othello

— many plays were performed at the Globe Theatre, one of London's most famous

— was in an acting troupe called Chamberlain's Men

— educated at the King Edward IV Grammar School in Stratford

— in school he studied Latin, Greek, and the Roman dramatists

— famous plays include *A Midsummer Night's Dream, Romeo and Juliet, Hamlet,* and *Macbeth*

— had three children: Susanna, Hamnet, and Judith

— Hamnet died in boyhood

— *Henry VIII* was his final play

— journeyed to London around 1585

— London theatres were closed from June 1592 to April 1594 because of the plague

3-65. AN INTERVIEW REPORT

You have interviewed Bobbette Blare, the famous rock star. Organize these 15 pieces of information that you took while conducting the interview. Then, on a separate piece of paper, write a report including all the information below. Use effective paragraphing, concise topic sentences, and logical sentence order and combinations.

— born in St. Louis, Missouri, on July 17, 1977

— has three brothers and one sister

— was voted "Most Likely to Make the Big Time" in her senior yearbook

— first sang on stage in her kindergarten recital, entitled "We Have Heart"

— plays guitar, piano, and harmonica

— has one hundred fifty different fan clubs

— both mother and father were professional singers

— has fourteen CDs that have been in the Top 40 CDs for the year

— was with her first band, Skyline Fever, for three years

— has traveled to 20 countries playing her music

— "My music touches many lives and I am grateful to all my terrific fans out there."

— enjoys doing charity shows whose proceeds go to the hungry and the homeless

— took piano and vocal lessons for ten years

— a frequent guest on late-night talk shows

— biggest hit, "Me and You," sold over two million copies

3-66. HOW TO DO AN ANALOGY QUESTION

An important type of writing assignment is the process essay. An important type of question on standardized tests is the analogy question. Here, the process essay and the analogy question meet. This following essay explains how to do an analogy question. Notice the main parts of the process essay—the introduction including the thesis statement, the several steps, presented chronologically, performed to answer the analogy, the necessary details, and the conclusion. Each paragraph features a particular phase of the process.

Directions: Read the following process essay and then, on a separate piece of paper, write a process essay about a process you know well. Shooting a foul shot, fixing a flat tire, programming a VCR, and playing a musical instrument are some suggestions. Include the same writing strategy and components employed in this essay. Share your process essay with your classmates.

The Analogy Problem

SKETCH : ARTIST as (a) painting : easel; (b) draft : writer; (c) pencil : architect; (d) blueprint : building

Answering an analogy question like the one above is not as difficult as some may think. After all, how hard is it to figure out how the word *sketch* and the word *artist* are related? It is not that difficult—if you know the correct method!

First, state how the two blackened words are related. You might say, "A sketch is a simple, rough drawing done by an artist." Then examine the choices looking for analogous relationships between the two words. These words in the possible choices do not have to have *similar meanings* to the words in darkened print. They must have *similar relationships* as the blackened pair. State the relationship between each pair of words in a sentence. Are any of the first words in the pairs, like a *draft* and a *writer*, something "simple and rough" and done by someone or something done by the second word in the pair? Now, eliminate word pairs that do not fit this relationship. If you have done this correctly, you see that answer (b) draft : writer has a similar relationship since a draft is a simple and rough writing done by a writer.

Sometimes, the process is not quite that simple. At times you might have to revise your relationship sentence to make it more specific and more exact to the blackened words' relationship. If you said, "An artist has a sketch," then you could also say, "An easel has a painting," "An architect has a pencil," and "A building has a blueprint," you would be somewhat correct, but these are not the desired relationships considering how a sketch and an artist are related.

Another consideration is the blackened words' part of speech. *Draft* is a noun and a verb. Since all the other pairs' first words are nouns, *draft* is probably a noun here. As a noun, it has several meanings. Look at the possible answers to see which definition of the word *draft* is most sensible. The "rough and simple" idea seems most appropriate.

Make sure you keep each pair's order the same. If a choice was "designer : blueprint," the relationship is similar to that of the blackened words, but the order is reversed. In order to be a good answer and have the same order as the original pair, the word *blueprint* should be listed first and the word *designer* should follow.

Thus, if you can understand the original pair's relationship, make up an exact sentence showing that relationship, review the possible answers, and eliminate the incorrect pairs, then you should do quite well in answering any analogy question!

3-67. THE COMPARISON-CONTRAST ESSAY

In writing a comparison–contrast essay, you show the reader how two subjects (people, places, events, objects, or the like) are similar and different. In this type of essay, the writer chooses to compare two places through a point-by-point comparison. The other technique is to compare them using a subject-by-subject comparison. In the following essay, notice the thesis statement, the order of comparison points, the specific details and examples, and the transitional phrases the writer chooses to show the similarities and differences of the two homes.

Directions: On a separate piece of paper, write your own comparison–contrast essay using the same techniques exemplified in the following essay.

A Tale of Two Places

I spent most of my early years living in a city apartment. When I turned fourteen, my family purchased a home in the suburbs. Though these two places have their similarities, they are also vastly different.

The homes themselves bore little resemblance to one another. We took the elevator up four flights to get to our apartment consisting of three bedrooms, a living room, a kitchen, and a bathroom. The three windows looked out onto a noisy street filled with cars, trucks, and buses. A constant parade of pedestrians was not uncommon, especially as these people walked along the sidewalks on their way to the subway station two blocks north of us. On the other hand, our seven-bedroom suburban home was situated on two acres in a wooded area miles away from the center of our town. Aside from the lawn mowers and leaf blowers, we seldom heard a motor, and we would often eat our meals as we watched the deer walk through our backyard.

Our activities in these two locations were also different. Our leisure time in the city was often spent on the playgrounds and in the many local museums. My friends and I played stickball, handball, and touch football in the city park or in the neighborhood school yard. We either walked or took the bus or subway to go anyplace. Yet, in the suburbs things were not the same. We generally played in our tree fort, romped up and down the hills of the local golf course, or rode our bicycles along the tree-lined streets. To get to our friends' house, we had to have mom or dad drive us since it was so far away.

The two schools I attended did not have much in common. P.S. 14 was a three-floor brick building lodged between a candy store and a cleaners. All students and most of the teachers either walked to school or took public transportation. At recess we played in a fenced-in asphalt court that had a few swings, a basketball hoop, and a seesaw. However, John Glenn Junior High School was quite different. The school, which sat upon a hill, had only one floor. Our gym classes were held in the field house or on the athletic fields consisting of three soccer fields, two softball fields, and a football field. The school district's own buses were parked in the bus garage behind the community auditorium.

Even though these two places were very different, each had its own special qualities.

3-68. THE CAUSE-AND-EFFECT ESSAY

The following essay is an interesting cause-and-effect personal essay showing how this young man became an outstanding basketball player. Notice the opening line used to grab the reader's attention, the important points he chose to relate to the reader, the sequential order of events, and the cause-and-effect connections. These combine to make an interesting, convincing cause-and-effect essay.

Directions: On a separate piece of paper, write your own cause-and-effect essay using the techniques use by this writer.

I cannot remember a day when I have not touched a basketball. There probably was a basketball in my hospital crib. Today basketball is my passion.

My father had always been a basketball fanatic. His basketball abilities earned him a full scholarship, and from there he went on to play in the Spanish Professional Basketball League. Many of my childhood days were spent in stuffy, smelly gyms watching my father practice with his talented teammates. Rather than just sit by bored, I started to dribble and shoot a basketball along the sidelines. With time, I became better and really started to enjoy the time spent practicing basketball. I was slowly getting hooked on the game of basketball!

When my father decided to hang up his basketball sneakers, he became my full-time basketball coach. He taught me the fundamentals including the proper techniques of dribbling, passing, rebounding, and defense. He pushed me to discipline my game and to outwork my opponents. These efforts were rewarded when I was selected for my junior high basketball team and actually started a few games at the end of the season. Coach Bergin presented me with The Lion's Award, a honor given to the team's most courageous player. This inspired me to work even harder since I had an outside chance at making the Varsity team as a tenth grader. With two summer camps, hours and hours of shooting, daily pickup games, and my father's patient, yet persistent coaching, I made the Varsity basketball team, my childhood dream!

My last two years playing high school basketball are memorable. Our team won the county championship, and after setting the county scoring record, I selected this college from many that offered me a full scholarship. With an even more determined effort, including seven days of practice for most of the school year, grueling hours in the weight room, and hundreds of miles up and down the basketball court, I was named both All-Conference and All-American. One sports magazine even called me "The Best College Basketball Player in America."

All these years of hard work have paid off and who knows what will happen in this year's National Basketball Association draft? Will I be selected in the first round? Will I be a lottery pick? Only time will tell.

3-69. A POWERFUL PARAGRAPH

In [1]*The Hunt and the Feast: A Life of Ernest Hemingway*, John Tessitore creates this memorable paragraph worth emulating. The author's sentence structure, diction, and syntax display the talents of a skilled writer. Mr. Tessitore's attention to detail adds strength to this paragraph. Lastly, his phrases and clauses help to create an interesting and enjoyable reading experience.

Directions: The paragraph's eleven sentences are numbered for you. On the lines provided, answer the ten questions regarding the paragraph. Include John Tessitore's techniques in your future writings.

(1) A person can rarely point to a moment in his life and say for sure that it, more than any other moment, shaped his entire future. **(2)** But for Ernest Hemingway, the night of June 7, 1918 provided one of those moments. **(3)** Lying in an exploded foxhole at a point on the Italian front nearest to enemy lines, with the sounds of battle erupting all around him, the nineteen-year-old Hemingway found the action for which he had been searching. **(4)** Weeks earlier, in his haste to join the war effort, he may not have considered all that war entailed. **(5)** But now, in the trenches, he knew what war was. **(6)** He had learned the hard way. **(7)** And he almost learned too late. **(8)** He was wounded, his legs were bleeding badly, and a dead man lay not three feet away. **(9)** Another man, also wounded, was moaning somewhere close by. **(10)** Heavy-artillery shells and machine-gun fire lit up the night sky. **(11)** Slipping in and out of consciousness, Hemingway had to wait for a friendly soldier to pull him out of no-man's-land.

1. What is the paragraph's purpose? _____

   _____

   _____

   _____

2. Which sentence is the paragraph's topic sentence? _____

3. Which two sentences begin with a participial phrase? _____ and _____

4. Which sentence contains examples of parallel structure? _____

5. Two sentences that begin with time transitions are (A) 1 and 10 (B) 4 and 5 (C) 7 and 8.

[1]Tessitore, John. *The Hunt and The Feast: A Life of Ernest Hemingway.* New York: Franklin Watts, 1996.

6. Cite three images found in sentences 8, 9, and 10 that show the horrors of war.

7. What is the purpose of the word *But* in the second sentence? _____

8. What is meant by the expression "no-man's-land" in the eleventh sentence? _____

9. Which two consecutive sentences are both simple sentences (sentences have one independent clause and no subordinate clauses)? _____ and _____

10. If the first sentence were not included in this paragraph, what would be lost?

3-70. THE DESCRIPTIVE ESSAY

Given the quotation, "In the dark time, the eye begins to see," student author Aaron Bronfman wrote this description of a man in deep reflection. Notice Aaron's descriptive techniques which include an interesting opening sentence, effective sensory details, intelligent diction, and mature sentence structure. On a separate piece of paper, use the same techniques to compose a descriptive essay about a person.

He sat in the darkness as images drifted before his eyes. He saw himself as a child, first embarrassed by his silver spoon but slowly made proud from taunts and gibes. That pride now welled up in him as he once again thought of his illustrious career. It was true, he had had a head start, but he had excelled far beyond what could be expected of a second-generation railway baron. He built his company into a global shipping power; for a time it was unrivaled in prestige and influence. So he thought again of defeated enemies and ruined competitors. That slow dock owner who had refused to sell, that old union leader who demanded "justice," even the crafty sultan with all of Persia behind him yielded at last. He was proud of the way he had seamlessly integrated smaller companies into his own, completely discarding those workers and managers who would not accept his view of the future. Thinking, too, of the alliances he had broken at the critical moment to gain dominance, he relished his victories; each one had its own delicious flavor.

He pursed his lips, and his brow furrowed in the darkness as his memory moved to more recent times. He recalled how the fall had begun; its speed was incomprehensible to him. Those rivals he had defeated saw the opportunity, and they exploited it. Businessmen greater than he dismantled his empire, piece-wise, until nothing was left. The situation was such that he could not find a single ally in the final days; no former colleague would risk association with him. He was so ruined by those last battles that he was left penniless. His great estate, the castle he had so lavishly furnished, was now without even electricity and telephone service. So he sat without light to see, and thinking of his rise and fall, realized at once his great mistake. "Oh, God, how could I have been so foolish?" he wondered woefully. "All this misery could have been spared me. Why was I so blind? Oh, Heaven, why did I not acquire that German conglomerate instead of the British one? Then it is true, as is said, 'In the dark time, the eye begins to see.'"

3-71. THE PERSUASIVE ESSAY

Using the poem "War" as your source material, compose a persuasive essay showing the negative effects of war. Organize your essay into several paragraphs, each having a topic sentence. Use a thesis statement to start the essay. Include many supportive details from the poem. Share your writings with your classmates.

War

"Attack"
Be prepared.
Could it be?
Did he hear correctly?
Everybody's on his own, again.
Fusillades fell quickly all around him.
Grenades and missiles filled the darkened skies.
Hit by the bullet, the soldier fell forward.
Injuries are all too common when wars are fought.
Justice, they say, is seldom found on these bloody battlefields.
Kindness, care, and concern for your enemy are scorned upon here.
Looking at his bloodied and shattered leg, the soldier began to cry.
Months of training for such a situation did not help him much now.
Never before had he felt such awful pain or wanted so much to live.
On many occasions he had imagined himself in this situation, struggling hard to stay alive.
"Perhaps," he thought, "this is how life and dreams will end, shattered on the battlefield."
Quietly, he thought about why he was here now, why he was dying, why he had lived.
Ruefully, the soldier began to prepare for death by giving in to the excruciating pain, hoping to die.
Slowly, this hurt began to slip away and a comfort, one that he had never felt before, overwhelmed him.
To die in such an inhumane way, bloodied and alone on this distant battlefield, was not what he had imagined.
Untimely death, unwarranted death, that death that poets and mystics acclaim and even revere, has the devil's print all over it.
Villainous leaders who seek to win glory for their country (and themselves) will never know who he was.
"When they bury me far from this horrible place," he thought, "they'll talk of honors and victories and all that kind of stuff."
"X" is my name to those men whose medals won't tell of the blood and guts and more we left here on the fields.
Youth has been wasted for the glory of the select few who spent the war in air-conditioned restaurants and slept comfortably through the air attacks.
Zero in, my friends, and know well this monster called war is a living hell that few of you will know as this dead soldier has.

Name _____ Date _____ Period _____

3-72. WRITING THE NARRATIVE

In this narrative, student writer Meredith McCloskey describes her college interview. Here she utilizes the traditional journalist's questions of Who? What? When? Where? Why? and How?. Additionally, using many sensory details and logical sequencing techniques, Meredith, through first-person narration, makes the reader experience the nervousness she felt at this time. Notice how the final event, another thought, effectively concludes the narration.

Directions: On a separate piece of paper, write your own narrative. Select an interesting experience or create a fictional one. Either way, use the same narrative techniques as found in the narrative below.

The Interview

As I sat across the table from this unfamiliar woman, I stared deeply into her brown eyes. "Please, just let me relax," I begged myself. My nervousness controlled my entire body. My mouth was so parched I could barely speak, and my tongue was as rough as a piece of sandpaper. My eyes could not focus; I was seeing a very blurry double of everything. I could hardly breathe; I felt as if I might fall to the floor.

When I heard the woman's placid voice as she smiled back at me almost begging me to calm down, my heart continued to race. It was only 11:35 A.M. There were still a good twenty minutes left in this brief visit to hell. I kept seeing these bright white flashes. "What is wrong with me?" I kept thinking. There was silence. I felt like something would just come to me, but the silence continued. Never before had I such a need for a stick of gum, a piece of candy, a wintergreen, a Tic Tac, a tiny sip of water—anything to make it easier to speak. Needless to say, I was having some difficulty in focusing.

Looking down at the red rug, I desperately tried to think of something intelligent to say. Eventually I came back to Earth and cleared my head enough to act somewhat normally for the rest of the conversation. By noon, I felt I could have talked for hours with this lovely woman.

When I left the interview, I looked for the nearest water fountain. Soon enough I returned to my usual somewhat clear state of mind. What was I so nervous about anyway? After all, it's only college . . . Why doesn't that make me feel better?

3-73. THE CLASSIFICATION ESSAY

A classification essay sorts individual items into categories. In the following essay, teachers are sorted into three categories (there could be many more) based on their teaching style. Ordered and logical, this classification essay shows how one member of a group (teachers) differs from another member of that same group. Notice the criterion the author uses to differentiate the three groups of teachers.

Directions: On a separate piece of paper, write a classification essay on a topic you select or one assigned by your teacher. Use the techniques employed in this classification essay.

The many thousands of school teachers in today's classrooms can be divided into three distinct types. Yes, they all instruct students, construct tests and quizzes, and assign grades. But how they do those tasks (and more) tells the difference.

All students would like to have a teacher like Miss Joy at least once in their academic career. She is bright, hardworking, congenial, challenging, and much more. Her lessons are informative and well-organized. The forty minutes breeze by. Miss Joy and other teachers like her make the subject more than interesting. Atticus Finch, Abraham Lincoln, and Marie Curie come to life in these classrooms. Discipline problems do not exist since students are kept productively busy. Plus no student would dare anger her since she is so kind and caring. As one student says, "I would never misbehave in Miss Joy's class. She is terrific. She is the best teacher in this school." With teachers like Miss Joy, students' grades are usually high since students perform to the best of their abilities, many times, in large measure, to please her.

Mr. Futziputts represents another type of teacher. He is the quintessential pushover. Discipline is not a word in his dictionary. Everybody can do want he or she wants because there is little or no discipline. Quizzes and tests, seldom given, are unchallenging. Constant threats concerning a "call home to your parents" and a "trip down to the principal's office" are seldom carried out. Students are allowed to do almost anything short of destroying the cinder-block walls in Mr. Futziputts's classroom. Very little academic work is done—either in the classroom or at home. Yet, somehow, everybody passes. Thank goodness there is no final state exam for Mr. Futziputts's class. Who knows how bad the results would be? Fortunately, most teachers like Mr. Futziputts are quickly found out and are usually asked to find other forms of employment.

Then there are teachers like Mr. Martinet. When students find out that he is their teacher, they know they must be on their best behavior. A former soldier, Mr. Martinet runs his class like an army regiment. "Don't be late or forget to hand in your homework," was one student's advice to her younger brother. Mr. Martinet is extremely well prepared for class. Conducted much like a strategy session, the lesson is organized, logical, and interesting. Students are always prepared and challenged. Most students, initially anxious in September, usually find in a short time that Mr. Martinet's classes are stimulating, satisfying, and strict! They learn much and are thankful for how Mr. Martinet made them "stand tall" to "smell the sweet scent of success."

Miss Joy, Mr. Futziputts, and Mr. Martinet are just a few of the different types of teachers charged with educating today's youth.

3-74. THE DEFINITION ESSAY

There are several ways to write a definition essay. The writer could give descriptive details, use narrative examples, compare, or contrast. Still, a combination of these four techniques would also constitute a definition essay. In the following definition essay, note the methods employed by the author. On a separate sheet of paper, write a definition essay using these methods or methods of your own choosing. Share your writing with your classmates.

Your Mother

She is that special woman who brought you into this world. She held you when you needed to be held. She cared for you late into the night when you were sick and needed that special TLC. She helped you learn to walk and taught you all the things a little child needs to learn—nursery rhymes, colors, how to sing, and how to draw. She watched *The Jungle Book* fifty-two times—and never alone! She taught you letters, and then words, and then sentences. She walked you to school on your first day and was waiting right outside the school door when that day was over. She helped you with your homework, wiped away frustration's tears, and cheered you when you played in the Peewee Division. She sat next to you on the piano bench and tenderly guided you through those seemingly unconquerable piano lesson pieces. She drove you to the mall and dropped you off a block away—at your request. She gave you advice concerning girlfriends and boyfriends. She confided in you as you did in her. She cried the day you entered high school much the way she did when you entered preschool and elementary school and middle school. She didn't think you saw those tears, but you did. She planned those family vacations and slept in the tent (without ever telling you how much her back hurt the following morning). She was the one in the front row of your school plays, your school music concerts, your school awards assemblies, and today, your high school graduation. She will also be the one in the front row at your wedding as you move on to your next stage in life. Yet, she has at least a hundred videotapes of you—never mind the countless number of pictures. She will not forget you—for you are, and always will be, her child. She is your mother.

3-75. AN ISOLATED HERO

John Tessitore, the author of [1]*The Hunt and the Feast: A Life of Ernest Hemingway*, begins his chapter entitled "An Isolated Hero" with the following paragraph. The opening paragraph of a book's chapter, a short story, or an essay is quite important. What does an author want to accomplish in the opening paragraph? Using Mr. Tessitore's skillfully constructed paragraph, you will review the components of an effectively written opening paragraph. Answer the questions on the lines provided. The sentences are numbered for easy reference.

(1) Besides the enormous success of *For Whom the Bell Tolls* in the early part of the decade, Ernest Hemingway received very little good news in the 1940s. **(2)** One by one the symbols of his youth were dropping away, leaving the energetic writer with a feeling of loneliness more severe than he had ever known. **(3)** Too old now for the fast-paced lifestyle he had made famous, but too stubborn to admit that those days were over, Hemingway found himself at the turning point of his life and his career. **(4)** But faced with the choice between a dignified old age and the action he had always craved, Hemingway was still choosing the action. **(5)** He was most alive on the battlefields, or on the hunt, or chasing a giant marlin through the Gulf of Mexico in *Pilar*. **(6)** Like the bullfighters in *Death in the Afternoon*, he was most alive when the action was life-threatening. **(7)** The safer, easier events of modern life only left him with time to think about his weakening powers as a writer and turned his attention to alcohol.

1. What is the purpose of the paragraph? _____

_____

_____

2. What specific evidence supports your answer to the previous question?

_____

_____

3. Why does Mr. Tessitore begin sentence 4 with the word *But*?

_____

_____

4. Authors use participial phrases to include information about the sentence's subject and to vary the types of sentences within the paragraph. Which sentence begins with consecutive participial phrases?

_____

_____

[1]Tessitore, John. *The Hunt and The Feast : A Life of Ernest Hemingway*. New York: Franklin Watts, 1996.

5. Paraphrase the paragraph's concluding sentence.

_____

_____

_____

6. What writer's tool is used in sentence 5?

_____

_____

_____

7. What is ironic about the chapter's title?

_____

_____

_____

8. Mr. Tessitore cites two connections between Hemingway's life and Hemingway's work as an author. What are those two examples?

_____

_____

_____

_____

9. List four adjectives that exemplify Hemingway as portrayed in this paragraph. Do not use any of the adjectives found within the paragraph itself.

_____

_____

_____

10. What do you think is the subject matter of the rest of this chapter?

_____

_____

_____

_____

IMAGING THINGS

3-76. I AM LIKE...

Have you ever compared yourself to an object, a place, an idea? Are you more like Paris or Miami? Are you more like the summer or the winter? Are you like a fox or a pussycat? Here is your chance to reveal those similarities.

Directions: Select two things, places, animals, vehicles, or others. In a paragraph each, show how you two are similar. Read the example paragraph in which the writer compares herself to the sun. That may help you in your decision and paragraph writing.

> **The Sun**
> I am like the sun. Both of us are warm and make people happy. Yet, both of us can burn if you don't watch out! At times the sun is easy to see, obvious to anyone who looks. I am that way too. Sometimes I like to be where everyone can see me. But at other times, like the sun, I am hiding from others. These are the moods I go through. Like the sun, I am happiest and glowing in the summer. This is when we both show up at the beach and enjoy the day!

First paragraph's title: _____

_____

_____

_____

_____

_____

_____

_____

Second paragraph's title: _____

_____

_____

_____

_____

_____

_____

_____

_____

3-77. A DAY IN THE LIFE

Fiction is in! Today you will become a clarinet, a streetlight, a hairbrush, or something more exotic—perhaps a computer. Using your five senses—sight, touch, smell, taste, and hearing—recreate a day in the life of an object (*not* a person) of your choice or one that is suggested below. Be specific and relate the details of such a day. The composition, whose length is specified by your teacher, can be serious or humorous. The goal is to use as many sensory images as you can to make the reader feel he or she is that object. Write your composition on the lines provided for you.

> **Suggestions:** iron, piece of chalk, mirror, window blinds, pocketbook or wallet, pen, hands, key, stapler, basketball, ear . . .

_____

_____

_____

_____

_____

_____

_____

_____

_____

_____

_____

_____

_____

_____

_____

_____

_____

3-78. DESCRIBING A PLACE

On the lines below, describe one of your favorite places. Include at least five adjectives, five specific verbs, three adverbs, and three conjunctions. Include at least three senses in your descriptions. Include two similes. Decide on the order of spatial details—large to small, distant to near, or some other arrangement. State your thesis statement directly. Include both objective descriptions using impersonal words, such as *tall* and *large* (focus on the place itself), and subjective descriptions (your personal reactions to the place). Decide on the number of paragraphs you will use. (Use the back of this sheet to continue your descriptions.)

_____

_____

_____

_____

_____

_____

_____

_____

_____

_____

_____

_____

_____

_____

_____

_____

_____

_____

_____

3-79. DEAR ADVICE COLUMNIST

Have you ever wished you could be an advice columnist helping people with their problems? Here is your chance to become the next Dear Abby or Ann Landers. On the appropriate lines, respond to these three problems with sensible solutions to solve the person's dilemma. Observing the rules of acceptable English, write your advice in well-written, interesting sentences. Share your pieces of advice with your classmates. Use the back of the page, if necessary.

Dear _____,
My father attends all my sporting events both on my school team and my town's club team. The problem is that he is very loud at these games. He lets the referees know when he thinks they have made a bad call. Additionally, he screams across the field giving me "tips" on how to play the game. Because he embarrasses me, I feel very uncomfortable with him at these games. How can I let him know how I feel without hurting his feelings?

_____

_____

_____

_____

Dear _____,
On the day before our science test, two people in my science class spotted the answer key for the following day's test. As one boy distracted the teacher, the other one took the answer key. Later that day, he passed the answers along to some others in the class. After our teacher scored the test, the average grade of those who had the answers before the test was 90%. For those who did not have the answers, the average grade was 74%. My score of 76% was earned without the help of the answer key. What should I do?

_____

_____

_____

_____

Dear _____,
I would like to ask this girl in my English class to the next school dance, but I can't get up the guts to invite her. It never seems to be the right time. I don't think calling her on the phone is the right way to ask her. What do you think I should do?

_____

_____

_____

_____

3-80. MAPPING A PARAGRAPH

There are some interesting requirements in the paragraph you will write on the lines below. Include three adverbs, three proper nouns, three conjunctions, three pronouns, three verbs beginning with the letter c, three prepositional phrases, and three colors. Underline each of these items in your paragraph. What you choose as your topic and what other information is included within the paragraph is your decision. Be interesting and have some fun!

_____

_____

_____

_____

_____

_____

_____

_____

_____

_____

_____

_____

_____

_____

_____

_____

_____

_____

_____

_____

_____

_____

_____

3-81. ARIZONA FACTS

Fifteen facts about Arizona, recorded in note-taking form, are found below. Organize the facts into logical sub-topics and then write a composition using these 15 facts. Use your own paper for the composition writing.

- 6th out of 50 states in total area

- capital city is Phoenix—the business and transportation center of the state

- entered the Union on Feb. 14, 1912, as the 48th state

- located in southwest United States

- bordered by California to the west and Mexico to the south

- Arizona means "few springs" (from the Indian word)

- geographic features include Mexican Highlands, the Colorado Plateau, the Colorado River, and the Grand Canyon

- climate varies with elevation

- Phoenix can average more than 100 degrees in the summer

- Phoenix can have below-freezing temperatures during the winter

- once depended on cotton, copper, and cattle

- manufacturing contributes mostly to today's economy (more than farming and mining)

- tourism is Arizona's second largest industry

- largest single employer is the federal government

- physical attractions include the Grand Canyon, the Painted Desert, the Petrified Forest—and engineering wonders Hoover Dam and Lake Mead

3-82. WRITING DIRECTIONS

Writing directions is an exact science. The writers must be totally aware of each step involved in the process. One mistake and the process breaks down. If you have ever received bad directions to a location and were lost because of them, you know how important exactness is.

This activity asks you to select one of the five processes and give a step-by-step set of directions on how it is to be done properly. Write your answers below and continue on the reverse side, if necessary. Check your steps before submitting them as answers. You don't want to be the cause of another's dilemma! An example set of directions is found below. You may use this same format for your response.

How to Make Popcorn

1. Place a two-quart pot (without its cover) on one of the stove's burners.
2. Pour 1/4 cup of cooking oil into the pot.
3. Pour enough kernels of corn to cover the pot's bottom.
4. Place the cover on the pot.
5. Turn the stove's appropriate burner on HIGH.
6. When the oil starts to sizzle, shake the pot gently on the stove's burner.
7. Continue shaking the pot in this manner until the kernels stop popping.
8. Turn off the stove and remove the pot from the hot burner immediately.
9. To prevent burns, cover the hot burner with a pot of water.
10. After a few minutes, pour the popcorn from the pot into a bowl.
11. Add salt to suit your taste.

Choose one of these five processes and write the directions to successfully complete the process: (a) How to tie a shoe; (b) How to fry an egg; (c) How to shoot a foul shot; (d) How to wrap a present; (e) How to blow a bubble with bubble gum.

_____

_____

_____

_____

_____

_____

_____

3-83. AN EXPERIENCE WITH QUOTATIONS

Select one of the following five quotations by famous people. On the line labeled "Explanation," tell what the quotation means to you. Then write an illustrative paragraph in which you exemplify how that quotation was true in a personal experience or one that happened to another person or group of people. The incident can be fiction or nonfiction. Perhaps a character from a novel, full-length play, or short story could be used. Within your paragraph, include and underline at least three nouns, three pronouns, three verbs, three adjectives, three adverbs, two prepositions, and one conjunction.

1. "Human beings are compelled to live within a lie, but they are compelled to do so only because they are in fact capable of living in this way." —*Vaclav Havel*

2. "In this world a man must either be an anvil or a hammer." —*Henry Wadsworth Longfellow*

3. "Every man is the architect of his own fortune." —*Sallust*

4. "No, when the fight begins within himself, a man's worth something." —*Robert Browning*

5. "Our greatest evils flow from ourselves." —*Jean-Jacques Rousseau*

Explanation _____

_____

_____

_____

Write your paragraph here.

_____

_____

_____

_____

_____

_____

_____

_____

_____

_____

3-84. YOUR IDEAS ABOUT TELEVISION AND THE MOVIES

Here is your chance to utilize your television- and movie-watching time. Select one of the four quotations below. Then select one television program and one movie that you will use as evidence in defending or arguing against the quotation. In each paragraph, underline your thesis statement and write the letters *SE* (for supporting evidence) before the sentence(s) that introduce a supporting point of evidence in your argument. Use at least two supporting points of evidence within each paragraph. Remember that the titles of television programs and movies are underlined. Write the paragraphs in the appropriate spaces below.

(A) "Life is made up of sobs, sniffles, and smiles with sniffles predominating."   —*O. Henry*

(B) "Man is not the creature of circumstances. Circumstances are the creatures of men." —*Benjamin Disraeli*

(C) "Man never reasons so much and so introspective as when he suffers."   —*Luigi Pirandello*

(D) "Our failings sometimes bind us to one another as closely as could virtue itself." —*Vauvenargues*

Write your paragraph about the television program here.

_____

_____

_____

_____

Write your paragraph about the movie here.

_____

_____

_____

_____

_____

_____

_____

3-85. POINT OF VIEW THROUGH AN INTERIOR MONOLOGUE

How would a parent view his or her child's kindergarten graduation? Would it be different from the way the child views it or how the child's grandparents view it? How are these perspectives different? By getting into the mind and emotions of each person, a good writer is able to express these different perspectives. An interior monologue, recording a person's thoughts in a narrative form, is one way to see a situation from a particular person's perspective.

Directions: Select an event and show the perspectives of three different people. Write your interior monologues on the appropriate lines. Share your ideas with your classmates.

The event is _____.

The first person is _____. Here is his/her interior monologue:

_____

_____

_____

_____

_____

_____

The second person is _____. Here is his/her interior monologue:

_____

_____

_____

_____

_____

_____

The third person is _____. Here is his/her interior monologue:

_____

_____

_____

_____

_____

_____

3-86. WOULD YOU RATHER...

Circle your choice in each pair. Then on a separate sheet of paper list three reasons why you made that choice. Then select one of the choices and write a 200-word story that relates, in some way, to your choice. The story can be fictional or factual. Use good details and diction.

1. Would you rather win $10,000 in the lottery **or** be guaranteed a happy life?

2. Would you prefer a month's vacation in New York City **or** Hawaii?

3. Do you want to be better looking **or** smarter than you are now?

4. If it came down to health **versus** wealth, which would you select?

5. Who should be paid more—a professional athlete **or** a lawyer **or** a country's leader?

6. Would you rather find a cure for cancer **or** write the all-time #1 bestselling novel?

7. When you graduate high school, would you like to have ranked number one academically in your class **or** have been selected the MVP in two varsity sports that year?

8. Would you prefer to live in the city **or** the country?

9. What is the world's most important invention?

10. Would you rather be the world's most popular musician **or** the world's most popular actor?

_____

_____

_____

_____

_____

_____

_____

_____

_____

_____

_____

_____

_____

(Continue on the back of this sheet.)

3-87. YESTERDAY, TODAY, AND TOMORROW

Do you enjoy being a teen during this time in history? Did the teens of one hundred years ago have it better? Do you think it will be better for teens one hundred years from today? Why? On the lines below, write a paragraph for each of these historical periods. In each paragraph, state two pros and two cons for that time. Discuss your thoughts with your classmates.

One hundred years ago:_____

_____

_____

_____

_____

_____

_____

_____

Today: _____

_____

_____

_____

_____

_____

_____

_____

One hundred years from today: _____

_____

_____

_____

_____

_____

_____

_____

3-88. SURPRISE!

Pretend that it is your 50th birthday and your friends have thrown a surprise party for you. One friend has written a speech highlighting your personality traits, your accomplishments, and other aspects of your life. Some of them are quite humorous!

Directions: Imagine that you could write that speech. What information would you include? Today is your chance to do exactly that. On the lines below, write that speech using good topic organization, effective sentences, and interesting details. Have a strong opening and a clever ending, as most speeches do. Most of all, have fun . . . and Happy Birthday!

_____

_____

_____

_____

_____

_____

_____

_____

_____

_____

_____

_____

_____

_____

_____

_____

_____

_____

_____

3-89. DESCRIBING A FRIEND

Select one of your friends. Now think about what personal traits he or she has that make you like him or her. Below is a list of traits that may help you in describing your friend. Choose any four of these adjectives or use some of them and add some of your own. Then, on a separate piece of paper, write a six-paragraph composition describing your friend. The first paragraph should include your friend's name and his or her four traits. The second paragraph's topic sentence includes the first trait you will discuss. An example or two should be offered as supportive evidence of that trait. The next three paragraphs should follow the same format as the second paragraph except that you will be discussing a different trait in each paragraph. The sixth paragraph will be brief and sum up, in no more than two or three sentences, the information found in the preceding paragraphs.

athletic	happy	opinionated
caring	hardworking	patient
considerate	humorous	polite
courageous	intelligent	pretty
creative	interesting	reliable
dramatic	kind	sophisticated
generous	loyal	tolerant
handsome	open-minded	trustworthy

3-90. A REAL TEST OF YOUR WRITING SKILLS

You decide what you would like to write about today. Then include the following 22 specifics within your composition. Each of the requirements is numbered and you should do the same in your writing. In this way, you and your teacher can check these items more efficiently. These items may appear anywhere in the composition as long as they flow well into the sense of the story.

1. the prepositional phrase *into the bank*
2. the prepositional phrase *after the party*
3. the prepositional phrase *near the car*
4. the adverb *carefully*
5. the adverb *loosely*
6. the adverb *savagely*
7. the adjective *tall*
8. the adjective *unwanted*
9. the adjective *secure*
10. the conjunction *and*
11. the conjunction *but*
12. the conjunction *or*
13. the color *green*
14. the color *red*
15. the color *white*
16. the pronoun *he*
17. the pronoun *them*
18. the pronoun *ourselves*
19. the clause *that Jill brought with her*
20. the word *Monday*
21. the word *September*
22. the number *five*

ANSWER KEYS

3-1. IDENTIFYING THE PARTS OF SPEECH

1. p—prep—adj—n—v—adj—prep—adj—adj—n.
2. adv—v—p—v—adj—adj—n—p—v—p?
3. p—c—p—v—v—adj—n—c—p—v—p/adj—n.
4. v—p—c—v—p—adj—n—adv—adj—n—v—prep—p/adj—n.
5. adj—n—v—v—prep—adj—adj—n—prep—adj—n.
6. p—v—v—adj—n—adv.
7. c—n—c—p/adj—n—v—v—p/adj—adj—n.
8. p—v—adv—v—p/adj—n—v—adv—prep—adj—n.
9. v—p—prep—adj—n—c—p—v—adv—prep—adj—n.
10. p—v—prep—p—p—adj—adv—adj—n—prep—p/adj—n—v—v.

3-2. PARTS-OF-SPEECH REVIEW

1. p—v—prep—adj—n.
2. v—p—v—p/adj—n?
3. v—p—adv.
4. p—v—adv—v—adj—n.
5. n—c—p—v—adj—n.
6. i—p/adj—n—v—v.
7. adj—n—v—adj—c—adj.
8. v—p—c—p—adv—v—n—adv?
9. v—adj—n.
10. c—p—v—adj—p—v—v—prep—n—adv.
11. p—v—p/adj—n—c—v—p/adj—n.
12. adv—v—p—v?

3-3. PARTS-OF-SPEECH REVIEW CROSSWORD PUZZLE

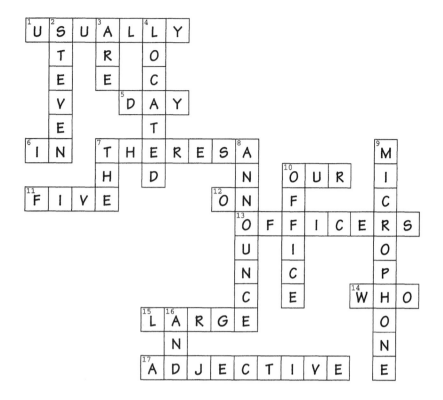

3-4. PLACING THE PUNCTUATION MARKS IN THEIR PROPER PLACES

1. "This is the first day of the rest of your life," a wise man once told me.
2. "What do you intend to do with your future?" he asked me.
3. Though some think life a chore, you should not.
4. There's so much to do each day; life is a present to be enjoyed.
5. Many people do not realize how precious life is.
6. Some others live by the proverb: *life's moments are momentous.*
7. Life is—shall I say—a beautiful experience.
8. The wise man then made this statement: "I have lived my life to the fullest."
9. "What have I taught you?" the wise man asked me before he left.
10. "Carpe diem!" I exclaimed.

3-5. REVIEWING PUNCTUATION MARKS

1. E	6. G
2. J	7. B
3. I	8. H
4. A	9. C
5. F	10. D

3-6.   JUMBLED SENTENCES

1. The chicken crossed the street.
2. Nancy listened to her recordings.
3. Our choir sang for the assembly.
4. She pushed down on the car's brake.
5. Bring back the joy in my life.
6. There is no frigate like a book.
7. Sharon was hired to restructure the committee.
8. They welcomed us back home.
9. What is the exact location of your store?
10. This is too good to be true!
11. It is very difficult to have a perfect score.
12. I am glad to be with you on your birthday.

3-7.   TURNING FRAGMENTS INTO SENTENCES

Answers will vary.

3-8.   HOW TASTY!

The phrases are 2, 5, 8, 11, and 15. They spell out ARTIFICIAL.
The clauses are 1, 4, 9, 12, and 13. They spell out SWEETENERS.
The sentences are numbers 3, 6, 7, 10, and 14. They spell out SACCHARINE.

3-9.   EACH HAS 40

The sentences are 1, 6, 7, 12, and 14.
The fragments are 3, 5, 8, 11, and 13.
The run-ons are 2, 4, 9, 10, and 15.

3-10.   MISTAKES . . . MISTAKES . . . MISTAKES

These are acceptable corrections:

1. I am not tired.
2. He ate a pretzel during the concert.
3. She is the taller of the two Thompson sisters.

4. You and he are the champions of the tournament.

5. He brought it here to our house yesterday.

6. Are they going home now?

7. Don't they remember our house number?

8. Gina, this problem about cheating on the test is the most difficult one of all.

9. He was driving past the largest mall in the state.

10. There is no such thing!

11. Since Josie is our chosen leader, we listen to her.

12. Some of the pepperoni pizza has been eaten. (Some of the pepperoni pizzas have been eaten.)

13. One of the students is selected to be chairperson each month.

14. Wednesday is her favorite day of the week.

15. Stop this racket immediately!

3-11.   13 ERRORS

1. past

2. No errors

3. Fragment: The hurricane had winds nearing one hundred fifteen miles per hour.

4. There is no comma after the word *experienced*. There is no need for the dash after the word *hurricanes*.

5. twenty-four   forecasters,

6. coast

7. No errors

8. Fragment: Surfing was allowed in some areas.

9. Tides were exceptionally high. Waves were three to six feet above normal.

10. No errors

11. taught   are

12. paramount

13. No errors

3-12.   THE BACKYARD EXPERIENCE

These are acceptable corrections:

While I sit in my backyard, I can hear the neighbors playing in their swimming pool. The young boys, Danny and Phil, are my neighbor's nephews. They are playing games such as Wave Pool, Marco Polo, Hold Your Breath, and Find the Coin. Danny's father, Robert, is also playing. He does not try very hard because he wants his sons to win. Danny had hurt his hand when he tagged his dad during the game of Tag. He is crying and his father is ineffectively trying to comfort him. So Danny leaves the pool and decides to eat hamburgers and hot dogs. Phil, the younger brother, and his dad also leave the pool to eat because they are hungry after playing in the pool for over an hour. The rest of the relatives are enjoying their supper and invite me over to join them. I politely refuse saying I am going to eat my supper with my wife and children in a few minutes.

3-13.   THE PARAGRAPH THAT NEEDS MUCH WORK

These are acceptable corrections:

The last time I saw Juan he was waving good-bye from the plane taking him to his native Spain. Juan had lived with a family in our town when he was an exchange student two years ago. He was in my social studies class and we struck up an immediate friendship. Both of us liked the same kinds of music, and we were starters on the soccer team that won the county championship. Seldom homesick, Juan adapted well to our country's customs. He fell in love with the many international restaurants in the city only thirty minutes away from us. Wanting to be a traveling journalist, Juan took several language courses and spoke with many people hoping to become more fluent in the language. Assuredly, he will be a success in his chosen field because he works so diligently. I hope to visit Juan and his family in Madrid this summer.

3-14.   THE ERROR DETECTOR

1. K	8. J
2. B	9. I
3. E	10. M
4. G	11. C
5. L	12. F
6. A	13. H
7. D	

The verb is BEG; the adjective is GLAD; the boy's name is JIM.

3-15.   MATCHING ERRORS AND EXAMPLES

1. G	8. P	12. C	16. M
2. R	9. L	13. H	17. D
3. A	10. O	14. E	
4. V	11. W	15. F	
5. I			
6. T			
7. Y			

The words are GRAVITY, PLOW, and CHEF. The abbreviation is MD (Medical Doctor).

3-16.   BY THE NUMBERS

The sentences are 2, 3, 6, 8, and 10.

3-17. ALL 26

sheriff	bazaar
background	talkative
wayward	landmark
flexible	excessively
lymph	acquire
unnecessary	apparel
monopoly	conceive
mechanical	merchant
intention	omission
hijack	grizzly
rabbit	precious
diesel	wonderful
immaculate	
bookkeeper	

3-18.   FOLLOWING YOUR TEACHER'S DIRECTIONS

These are possible answers.

1. I can hardly see you.
2. This is the easiest way to finish the task.
3. The elephant, walking aimlessly around the ring, was out of sorts.
4. Take this package to Mrs. Kennedy's apartment.
5. We will read this information later when we are not so busy.
6. Mr. Bucci, our friendly neighbor, is the new fire chief.
7. Your numerical method is helpful.
8. Missy is the most talented skater and her team will tour this summer.
9. The doctor thanked her patients for their patience.
10. I carry my identification and credit cards in this wallet, my birthday present.
11. The couple strolled along the shore.
12. A bathing suit and towel are all you need.
13. If he can read, he can comprehend this text.
14. Grandpa could see the towels rotating in the clothes dryer.
15. We guys (or We) can help you restructure the garage.

3-19. COMBINING SENTENCES

These are possible combined sentences.

1. Hugh is intelligent, interesting, and kind.

2. The approaching storm, Hurricane Bonnie, will hit somewhere in North Carolina.

3. The scissors with white handles that Kate used to cut Jamey's hair were found on the desk.

4. Joe called his hardworking editor, Marcia, at Sundial Books.

5. Born on November 11, 1974, Leonardo DiCaprio, an only child, was named after Renaissance artist Leonardo Da Vinci.

6. Currently being recruited by many Division I colleges, Jocelyn, an A student and varsity basketball player, wants to be a dentist.

7. Propene, an alkene, has three carbon atoms and six hydrogen atoms.

8. The Marshall Plan, passed by Congress in 1947, is named after George C. Marshall, the U.S. Secretary of State, who proposed a way that the United States could strengthen Europe's economy after World War II.

9. Born in Allegheny, Pennsylvania in 1874, Gertrude Stein, the author of <u>The Autobiography of Alice B. Toklas</u>, loved to read the plays of William Shakespeare.

10. Because the class was talking, the substitute teacher assigned a composition that she said would count as a test grade.

3-20.   METHODS OF TRANSPORTATION

The completed sentences with their methods of transportation are as follows.

1. The movie producer specializes in films concerning race relations. **(planes)**

2. The rebel leader has promised to overthrow the government. **(trains)**

3. The state's courtroom was packed with photographers and reporters. **(trolleys)**

4. Many of the ships had to pass through the Panama Canal. **(autos)**

5. The suspended player was not permitted to sit in the team's dugout. **(sleds)**

6. Several workers asked their boss for an extra hour's pay. **(skates)**

7. Do you think that the new rules will be accepted by the students? **(gondolas)**

8. After he completed the paint job, he washed the brushes and stored the cans. **(surfboards)**

9. Without a helmet the cyclist is asking for trouble. **(canoes)**

10. The benign tumor was removed by the skilled surgeon. **(carriages)**

3-21.   PLACING THE PARTICIPLES PROPERLY

1. I	9. D
2. J	10. G
3. H	11. K
4. F	12. A
5. L	13. E
6. C	14. N
7. O	15. M
8. B	

3-22.   A DIFFERENT KIND OF PARAGRAPH

Answers will vary. Here is a sample paragraph.

Today was not the best day of my life. First, my alarm clock did not go off. Then, because our hot water was not working properly, I was forced to take a cold shower. Breakfast was not much better since we had run out of milk. Just when I thought things could not get worse, they did. Since my bus had already come and gone, I took a cab to school. Eight dollars later, I arrived at school having already missed first period and late for second period. There Mr. Ambrose, our social studies teacher, sprang a quiz on us. Only two students passed; needless to say, I was not one of them. Later, Justin Holiday, my lab partner, said Mrs. Loftin would not accept our lab report since it did not have the proper heading. Luckily, the last period arrived and we were given a study hall by our French teacher, Madame Roget, who said she had had such a bad day that she just needed to rest a bit. Should I tell her about my day? I think not!

3-23.   ORDER IN THE PARAGRAPH

Paragraph One: B, D, F, A, E, G, C
Paragraph Two: C, B, A, D, E

3-24.   TEN INTO ONE (TWICE)

Paragraphs will vary. These are samples:

First paragraph: With waves crashing on the shore, the couple walked along the shore, collecting shells. Pulling an advertisement, an airplane flew above them as fishermen checked their lines in the distance. Holding hands, the couple talked about their jobs as seagulls lined up on the shore, boats cruised out in the water, and children built sand castles.

Second paragraph: As an airplane pulling an advertisement flew above and fishermen checked their lines, a couple, holding hands, walked along the shore. They collected shells and talked about their jobs. At the same time, seagulls lined up along the shore and children built sand castles. While the waves crashed, boats cruised out in the water.

3-25. RESTORING ORDER

One paragraph: A, D, E, G, J, L
The other paragraph: B, C, F, H, I, K

3-26.   TRANSITIONAL WORDS AND PHRASES

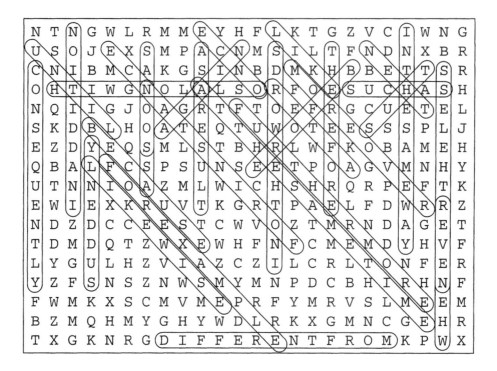

3-27.   MAKING THE DISTINCTION

Answers will vary.

3-28.   FACT VERSUS OPINION

1. F	6. F	11. O	16. O
2. O	7. O	12. O	17. F
3. F	8. F	13. O	18. O
4. O	9. O	14. O	19. O
5. O	10. O	15. F	20. O

3-29. DISTINGUISHING FACT FROM OPINION

Possible answers are as follows.

1. *Definition:* A VCR is an electronic machine that can tape and replay television shows and movies.

   Opinion: A VCR is one of the most amazing inventions of this century.

2. *Definition:* Group projects are assignments in which students are placed in groups to accomplish a certain task.

   Opinion: Group projects force the hardworking students to do not only their work but also the work of the less ambitious students within the group.

3. *Definition:* Monster movies are films in which a monster attempts to scare or destroy other creatures, people in particular.

   Opinion: Monster movies have become scarier due to improved film techniques.

4. *Definition:* Subways are a city's underground railway or the tunnels through which it runs.

   Opinion: My city's subways are safe and comfortable.

5. *Definition:* Monopoly® is a board game whose objective is to accumulate wealth primarily through real estate transactions.

   Opinion: Monopoly® offers intellectual challenges and enjoyment to its players.

6. *Definition:* A middle school is an educational facility housing students who have finished elementary school but have not started high school.

   Opinion: Middle school is a pleasant academic and social environment for an adolescent to mature intellectually and socially.

3-30. THE FACTS AND OPINIONS OF POETRY

1. FACT
2. FACT
3. FACT
4. FACT
5. BOTH
6. BOTH
7. OPINION
8. OPINION
9. OPINION
10. OPINION
11. OPINION
12. BOTH
13. BOTH
14. FACT
15. FACT

3-31. DEVELOPING TOPIC SENTENCES

Answers will vary.

3-32.   WORKING WITH TOPIC SENTENCES

The topic is listed first, followed by the attitude.

1. Jogging . . . helps people keep fit.
2. Richard . . . our most challenging opponent.
3. Cultural biases . . . are detrimental to a society's well-being.
4. Researching one's family history . . . is an eye-opening experience.
5. E-mail . . . is more exciting than postal mail.
6. Taxpayers . . . are anxious about their tax returns.
7. Atticus Finch . . . is one of literature's most memorable characters.
8. A day at the beach . . . is the most exhilarating experience for the Morton family.
9. The columnist's article . . . is a brilliant piece of journalism.
10. The lion . . . is the most interesting animal to study.
11. Discipline . . . is a necessity for success in life.
12. The Pine Barrens . . . should not be commercially developed.
13. Alfred Hitchcock . . . was one of the most talented movie directors.
14. Insignificant school rules . . . are troublesome.
15. Cancer detection . . . should remain one of the country's medical priorities.

3-33.   TOPIC SENTENCE REVIEW

Answers will vary.

3-34.   THE THESIS STATEMENT

Answers will vary.

3-35.   SUPPORTING YOUR THESIS STATEMENT

Answers will vary.

3-36.   GIVING GOOD REASONS

Answers will vary.

3-37.   EXPRESSING YOURSELF

Answers will vary.

3-38. SUPPORTING YOUR OPINIONS

Answers will vary.

3-39. SUPPORTING YOUR CHOICE

Answers will vary.

3-40. SUPPORTING YOURSELF ON SCHOOL ISSUES

Answers will vary.

3-41. TAKING A STAND ON LITERATURE

Answers will vary.

3-42. SELECT, STATE, AND NARROW

Answers will vary.

3-43. LISTING YOUR IDEAS

Answers will vary.

3-44. THINKING ABOUT TOPICS

Answers will vary.

3-45. DEVELOPING THE TOPIC

Answers may vary. These are examples.

1. a. analyze—what components make up the music of today
   b. argue—today's musical lyrics are more expressive in the open
   c. compare—today's musical lyrics vs. those of the 1950s
   d. evaluate—the merit of today's musical lyrics

2. a. argue—bad because more dependent on machines

    b. compare—life today vs. life at the turn of the 19th century

    c. describe—life with or without technology today

    d. narrate—tell the stories of two children who lived during those different times

3. a. argue—stressful and interesting

    b. compare—teen today vs. a teen in my grandparent's time

    c. describe—what a teen encounters today

    d. inform—let people know what demands and opportunities there are for teens today

4. a. analyze—goals and scope and sequence

    b. classify—academic/vocational/pre-college/undergraduate/graduate

    c. compare—today vs. fifty to sixty years ago

    d. narrate—story of a typical school week

3-46. A TOPIC'S DEVELOPMENT

These are possible answers. Students may argue for other answers as well.

1. D, E
2. I
3. A, F, H
4. A
5. C
6. D, E, F, G
7. B, C
8. A, E, H, I
9. E, F, G, H
10. A, H
11. I
12. B, C, G, H
13. B, C, G, H
14. A, G, F, H
15. D, E, H

3-47. PARAPHRASING

These are possible paraphrases:

1. The best gift you can give is yourself.
2. A good cook's food must be eaten moderately.

3. The truth is one's best defense.

4. Time heals feelings better than reason.

5. Everyone relies on him/her who is willing to help or do the work.

6. It is harder to keep a friendship than to make one.

7. One lie will destroy a thousand truths.

8. Since you can't win at everything, be happy with what you have done.

9. Anything goes in war.

10. Marriage is constricting.

3-48. REWORDING MEMORABLE WORDS

Possible paraphrases include the following:

1. Man is responsible for his personal situations.

2. Cheap things, initially inexpensive, will be costly in the long run.

3. Democracy is the best political system we have.

4. We create our own happiness.

5. It is neither honorable nor disgraceful to be poor.

6. One's reputation, often earned undeservedly, is an idle and false burden that is often lost undeservedly.

7. I cannot resist temptation.

8. Having no money is the worst predicament for a traveler.

9. Sticking with the painstaking toils of a vocation is the real test.

10. How one uses his riches is far more important than simply having those riches.

11. A writer must feel what he is writing if he expects his reader to do the same.

12. What starts out as friendship between two people often becomes love; but those two who fall out of love never stay friends.

3-49. SHOW US HOW THEY FEEL

Answers will vary.

3-50. LET'S GET EMOTIONAL

Answers will vary.

3-51. SHOWING THE CONTRASTS

Answers will vary.

3-52. WORKING WITH QUOTATIONS

1. existence
2. excess
3. heredity
4. reputation
5. competition

6. privacy
7. intelligence
8. tradition
9. consistency
10. bribery

3-53. WHAT IS THE DIFFERENCE?

Answers will vary.

3-54. ILLUSTRATIVE SENTENCES

Answers will vary.

3-55. USING THE CORRECT WORD

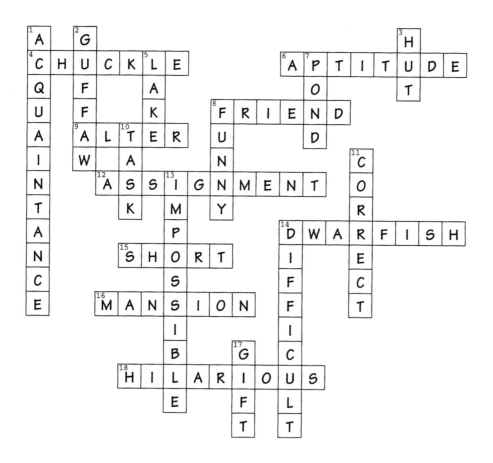

3-56. A SENSATIONAL ASSIGNMENT

Answers will vary.

3-57. NOTING AN AUTHOR'S OPINION

1. B	6. C	11. A	16. B
2. A/D	7. C	12. C	17. C
3. D	8. A	13. A	18. D
4. A	9. B	14. A	19. A
5. D	10. C	15. B	20. A

3-58. TIME OUT FOR SOME FUN WITH OXYMORONS

1. HE	12. ST
2. WH	13. SH
3. OD	14. AR
4. IV	15. EA
5. ID	16. SP
6. ES	17. AN
7. GE	18. IS
8. TS	19. HP
9. TH	20. RO
10. EW	21. VE
11. OR	22. RB

HE WHO DIVIDES GETS THE WORST SHARE.—A SPANISH PROVERB

3-59. TRACING THE SOURCE

1. ST	9. IN
2. AR	10. SP
3. TG	11. RI
4. EN	12. NG
5. ES	13. EM
6. IS	14. BR
7. OR	15. YO
8. IG	

Five synonyms for *source*: START, GENESIS, ORIGIN, SPRING, EMBRYO

3-60. IDIOMS

1. to listen to someone
2. tired; exhausted
3. almost everything
4. to daydream
5. bring the story to a close
6. get down to important business
7. to have things in the wrong order
8. take on a challenge
9. the same thing
10. improve one's situation
11. to satisfy
12. to ignore
13. to avoid saying something you would like to say
14. to work very hard
15. to trick
16. experienced
17. to move slowly
18. awkward
19. same types
20. pay the bill

3-61. SETTING DOWN THE TERMS

These are sample answers.

1. The audience is the intended readers, those the writer wants to reach.
2. Content is the material or information that makes up the paragraph, essay, or longer writing.
3. Writing forms are the types of writing that include expository (to present information), personal (to examine private issues), creative (to create poems, stories, plays, and more), persuasive (to argue your stance on an issue), and functional (to communicate everyday matters including business and personal matters).
4. The purpose of an essay is the written goal whether it be to inform, persuade, entertain, evaluate, propose, or other.
5. Clarity is the author's desired clearness of expression in thought and purpose.
6. Diction is the word choice, the appropriate language for the intended audience.
7. A fragment is a part of the sentence. A fragment does not include all three of the necessary sentence components, i.e., a subject, a predicate, and a complete thought.
8. A run-on is the incorrect fusion of two complete sentences. An example of a run-on is *Bertha ate the cake, she also drank some milk with the cake.*
9. A writer's voice is the sense of the author's character, personality, and attitude that comes through the words.
10. The writer's personal touch is the writer's own comments or experiences. These include the author's anecdotal descriptions.

3-62. SOME FOOD FOR THOUGHT REGARDING THE PARAGRAPH

1. beginning
2. subject; opinion

3. If a thesis statement is stated, it is written as a sentence within the paragraph. If a thesis statement is implied, it is not directly stated in the paragraph, but its sense is implied and the reader can infer what the thesis is though it is not stated directly.

4. The paragraph's content may require it to be placed elsewhere. A writer may choose to lead up to the topic sentence and place it either in the middle or near the end (possibly as the concluding sentence) of the paragraph.

5. Supporting sentences defend the writer's opinion. They are usually facts, though they can also be personal experience or opinions. If the writer chooses to defend the evils of smoking, for example, he or she can do so with facts showing the ill effects of smoking.

6. A fact is something that has actually happened. It is also a statistic that can be proven. "The robber entered the bank at two o'clock" is a fact, as long as it is true. An opinion is a belief. It is not necessarily supported by concrete evidence. The writer's statement "Skiing is fun" is an opinion.

7. (A) F; (B) O; (C) F; (D) O; (E) F

8. opinion

9. Our town's Memorial Day parade was memorable.

10. New York City has something for everybody.

3-63. DESCRIBING PEOPLE, PLACES, AND THINGS

Answers will vary.

3-64. WRITING A REPORT

Answers will vary.

3-65. AN INTERVIEW REPORT

Answers will vary.

3-66. HOW TO DO AN ANALOGY QUESTION

Answers will vary.

3-67. THE COMPARISON-CONTRAST ESSAY

Answers will vary.

3-68.   THE CAUSE-AND-EFFECT ESSAY

Answers will vary.

3-69.   A POWERFUL PARAGRAPH

1. The paragraph details a defining moment in Ernest Hemingway's life.
2. 1
3. 3 and 11
4. 8
5. (B) 4 and 5
6. The images showing war's horrors are "He was wounded, his legs were badly bleeding, and a dead man lay not three feet away (8). The wounded man in sentence nine is another example. Finally, the "heavy artillery shells and machine-gun fire" that "lit up the sky" (10) are other examples of war's horrors.
7. *But* adds emphasis and transition from sentence 1 to sentence 2 as the author cites how Hemingway had his defining moment on June 7, 1918.
8. Since Hemingway was "slipping in and out of consciousness," the reader can assume here that "no-man's-land" is a state of mental confusion.
9. Sentences 6 and 7 are simple sentences.
10. The paragraph is focused around the concept of a moment that shaped Hemingway's life. Eliminate the first sentence, and the central focus of the paragraph is lost.

3-70.   THE DESCRIPTIVE ESSAY

Answers will vary.

3-71.   THE PERSUASIVE ESSAY

Answers will vary.

3-72.   WRITING THE NARRATIVE

Answers will vary.

3-73.   THE CLASSIFICATION ESSAY

Answers will vary.

3-74. THE DEFINITION ESSAY

Answers will vary.

3-75. AN ISOLATED HERO

1. The paragraph depicts the change in Hemingway's success and actions. He was more lonely than ever before and at a turning point in his career where he had to choose action over inaction.
2. Sentences 5 and 6 recount Hemingway's activities.
3. The fourth sentence is the transition between Hemingway's inactive and active lifestyles.
4. Sentence 3 begins with consecutive participial phrases.
5. If Hemingway was not active, he would become somewhat depressed and drink alcohol.
6. Mr. Tessitore uses parallel structure showing three areas where Hemingway felt alive—on the battlefields, on the hunt, and through the Gulf of Mexico chasing a giant marlin.
7. The irony is that a hero is not normally perceived as isolated.
8. Hemingway was most alive when chasing a giant marlin through the Gulf of Mexico in *Pilar* and when he was in a life-threatening situation similar to the bullfighters in *Death in the Afternoon*.
9. Answers will vary, but may include lively, headstrong, vibrant, and courageous.
10. Answers will vary.

3-76. I AM LIKE . . .

Answers will vary.

3-77. A DAY IN THE LIFE

Answers will vary.

3-78. DESCRIBING A PLACE

Answers will vary.

3-79. DEAR ADVICE COLUMNIST

Answers will vary.

3-80. MAPPING A PARAGRAPH

Answers will vary.

3-81. ARIZONA FACTS

A possible composition format is as follows:

Arizona, the Indian word for "few springs," entered the Union on February 14, 1912, as the forty-eighth state. Located in the southwest United States, Arizona is bordered by California to the west and Mexico to the south. Arizona ranks sixth out of the fifty states in total area. Its capital city, Phoenix, is the business and transportation center of the state.

Arizona's geographical features, including the Mexican Highlands, the Colorado Plateau, the Colorado River, and the Grand Canyon, are interesting. Additional physical attractions are the Painted Desert, the Petrified Forest, and the engineering wonders of Hoover Dam and Lake Mead. The climate varies with the elevation. Phoenix can average more than one hundred degrees in the summer and can have below-freezing temperatures during the winter.

Though the Arizona population once depended on cotton, copper, and cattle for their primary income, today the federal government is the largest single employer. Tourism is Arizona's second largest industry. Additionally, manufacturing, more than farming and mining, contributes mostly to today's economy.

3-82. WRITING DIRECTIONS

Answers will vary.

3-83. AN EXPERIENCE WITH QUOTATIONS

Answers will vary.

3-84. YOUR IDEAS ABOUT TELEVISION AND THE MOVIES

Answers will vary.

3-85. POINT OF VIEW THROUGH AN INTERIOR MONOLOGUE

Answers will vary.

3-86.   WOULD YOU RATHER . . .

Answers will vary.

3-87.   YESTERDAY, TODAY, AND TOMORROW

Answers will vary.

3-88.   SURPRISE!

Answers will vary.

3-89.   DESCRIBING A FRIEND

Answers will vary.

3-90.   A REAL TEST OF YOUR WRITING SKILLS

Answers will vary.

I'M AWESOME.

HERE'S WHY...

110 Lists, Activities, and Prompts to
Remind You Why You're Amazing

SARA KATHERINE

Adams Media
New York London Toronto Sydney New Delhi

Adams Media
An Imprint of Simon & Schuster, Inc.
57 Littlefield Street
Avon, Massachusetts 02322

First Adams Media trade paperback edition April 2019

ADAMS MEDIA and colophon are trademarks of Simon & Schuster.

For information about special discounts for bulk purchases, please contact Simon & Schuster Special Sales at 1-866-506-1949 or business@simonandschuster.com.

The Simon & Schuster Speakers Bureau can bring authors to your live event. For more information or to book an event contact the Simon & Schuster Speakers Bureau at 1-866-248-3049 or visit our website at www.simonspeakers.com.

Interior design by Sylvia McArdle
Interior images © Getty Images and 123RF.com; images on pages 27, 70, 138, 139, 142, and 143 by Nicola DosSantos

Manufactured in the United States of America

10 9 8 7 6 5 4 3 2 1

Library of Congress Cataloging-in-Publication Data has been applied for.

ISBN 978-1-5072-0962-2
ISBN 978-1-5072-0963-9 (ebook)

DEDICATION

To my family, incredible boyfriend,
and amazing friends who help me feel
awesome every day.

CONTENTS

INTRODUCTION

YOU ARE AWESOME. Yes, really! Having a hard time remembering that? That's okay! From looking and dressing a certain way to earning X amount annually, there is a lot of pressure out there, self-imposed and otherwise, to be "perfect." And it may seem like you are the only one who is afraid of failing, or worried about whether you say the "right" things, look the "right" way, or act in the "right" manner. But this just isn't true! Everyone has their own personal struggles and doubts, just like you—so when will you recognize that you're capable, unique, and most importantly, awesome? That's where we come in.

I'm Awesome. Here's Why... is a crash course to finding beauty and confidence within yourself. You will discover more than one hundred guided activities to help you realize, build, and nurture your self-confidence, from illustrated prompts to affirmations of your awesomeness. You'll:

▶ Create a road map to explore your past accomplishments and visualize your dreams for the future.

▶ Fill in a trophy to celebrate your talents—no matter how big or small.

▶ Rid your closet of anything that makes you feel less than your awesome self.

You can work through these activities from beginning to end, or flip through to the activities that jump out at you. But before you dive in, check out Part 1 on self-confidence. Here, you'll discover just what it means, why it is so important, and what key issues may be holding you back from truly believing in yourself.

Anything you write here is for *you*. You're going to get deep, but have a lot of fun in the process. It's time to show—or remind—yourself what is beautiful and awesome about you!

CONFIDENCE BEGINS WITH YOU

What is self-confidence, and how can you can cultivate and improve your own confidence? This part is here to answer those questions—and more! You'll discover why self-confidence isn't necessarily an end goal, but more of a journey. You'll also learn about the six key elements involved in building self-esteem, including recognizing your strengths and weaknesses, practicing self-care, embracing failure, and building positive resilience.
So let's get started!

What Is Self-Confidence?

Something many people don't realize is that self-confidence isn't really a destination. You won't wake up one day having reached this point of always feeling confident and awesome about yourself all day, every day. It's simply not possible. As corny as it may sound, self-confidence is actually a continuous journey of resilience and self-discovery. Each day you work toward building more and more self-confidence, discovering so many awesome things you didn't know about yourself before. You might find out that you have a natural talent for something unexpected (like cooking French cuisine!), or maybe you'll find your passion in volunteering at an animal shelter! Each amazing part of you helps fill your internal well of self-love, and aids in your ability to handle anything that life may throw at you.

Everyone experiences self-doubt and uncertainty. Even those who may seem self-assured all the time will falter at certain points throughout their lives. There are a few common reasons for feeling this uncertainty throughout your life, including comparing yourself to others, experiencing failure, and setting unrealistically high expectations for yourself. Do any of these sound familiar? If so, you're not alone. It's normal to struggle with self-esteem when you're faced with these types of challenges.

Confidence is a constant work in progress, combining your perceptions about yourself with how you interpret and handle others' opinions of you. If you work toward strengthening your self-confidence throughout your life's journey, you'll realize that even the struggles that come with comparing yourself to others, experiencing failure, and setting unrealistic expectations are an important part of self-discovery and being the awesome person that you are. If you believe in yourself, you'll develop a much stronger sense of resilience and self-love.

But how do you reach this point?

Cultivating Self-Confidence

There are quite a few important elements that contribute to your ongoing self-confidence journey, from acknowledging your strengths and weaknesses, to learning how to take pride in yourself and prioritizing self-care. Each of these elements help you build a solid foundation, while ensuring that you are mindful of the beliefs, thoughts, or behaviors that may be limiting your self-confidence.

Recognize Your Strengths and Weaknesses

Many may believe that having a strong sense of self-confidence means focusing on your strengths and using them as much as possible. However, if you ignore your weaknesses, you'll never have a full sense of your entire self and your potential.

It's hard to truly understand who you are and how you can grow if you aren't aware of the areas that may need a little more attention. When you're truly self-aware, you can embrace all of your imperfections, and take the time to work on improving yourself in these areas. Plus, these weaknesses make you human. Everyone has them, so there's no reason to ignore or feel ashamed of these parts of who you are!

For example, say you've known that writing is a strength of yours ever since you were younger. You may feel very confident in your abilities, but it isn't until you are older that you realize one of your biggest weaknesses: your fear of failure.

At first, you may think that acknowledging this weakness isn't connected to your strengths in writing. However, when you start subconsciously making excuses to not write or procrastinate on a writing project, it's usually because you're afraid. You may be afraid of writing something bad, or that you'll experience writer's block and have no clue what to write about at all. Or perhaps you fear what people who read your writing will say.

The root of this procrastination and worry is your fear of failure. While writing is your strength, your fear of failure is keeping you from actually writing and also from feeling confident in the work you produce. Once you understand this connection, you will be able to find ways to overcome those fears in order to strengthen both your writing skills and your confidence in these abilities. Fears and insecurities like these are something you will need to work on every day. They are a continuous work in progress, just like your journey toward self-confidence and loving your awesome self.

TAKE PRIDE IN YOURSELF

Can you really be self-confident if you aren't proud of yourself? Feeling proud of yourself is often very difficult for someone who struggles with self-confidence. However, there's so much you can be proud of—even if you don't realize it yet! You're here, right? You're taking the time to learn and grow by choosing to read this book. You might be rolling your eyes, but it's truly an accomplishment to be able to do this. Many people struggle with taking the first step toward improving themselves and their current situation. By choosing to read this book, you're already ahead! That's pretty awesome. Having a sense of pride in yourself will push you forward when times get tough, allowing you to believe that you have what it takes in order to overcome these challenges. After all, how can you face these difficult roadblocks if you don't believe in yourself?

One challenge in feeling proud of yourself is when you start comparing yourself to others. Nowadays, this is mainly due to how constant and expansive the surge of social media is. When everyone is using social media to showcase the best parts of their lives, it's extremely easy to get stuck in a comparison trap and feel as though you don't measure up. When you find yourself stuck in one of these traps, take a social media detox for a bit. If you're struggling to completely cut yourself off from social media, start by allowing yourself shorter increments of online time. Keep track of the time, and don't let yourself log back on when your allotted time is up.

Another good practice when you're struggling to feel proud of yourself is to look back at some of the goals or tasks you've accomplished in the past. No matter how big or small, every achievement in your life is important, and is a huge part of what makes you the awesome human you are today.

PRACTICE SELF-CARE

While self-care practices are primarily seen as a part of improving your health, they also play an important part in building your self-confidence. Self-love is an integral part of self-care, expressing kindness and appreciation for yourself by nurturing your body, mind, and soul in ways that leave you feeling rejuvenated.

The foundation of self-care is treating yourself with the kindness and respect you deserve. It's about listening to your body, mind, and heart and paying attention to what they crave. You may think of it as each part having its own bucket. When these buckets are full, *you* feel full. When you're filling these buckets regularly, you simply *feel* more confident, and have a much higher chance of achieving your dreams.

Think about what activities help your body feel good, improve your mental health, and help you flourish. For your body, it can be as simple as eating nutrient-rich foods, exercising regularly, or resting when you're tired. Some easy habits to improve your mental health include meditation, yoga, and surrounding yourself with positive things and people. You can also dig deeper: perhaps there is a relationship in your life that is not beneficial, or there are situations where you may need to set boundaries and practice putting yourself first when needed. Finally, self-care includes participating in activities that simply make you feel *good*. What do you truly love to do? What sparks happiness in your life? Make time to participate in things that bring you joy.

Since this is a rather quick lesson in self-care, you can find more information through the resources in the Appendix. Also, take the time to listen to what the inner well of your self needs, and don't forget to put yourself first sometimes. In the end, it'll help you feel *awesome*.

EMBRACE FAILURE

In order to fully feel confident in yourself, you can't be afraid of failure. Sure, it feels great when everything works out perfectly the first time, but the truth is that failure comes with success. One quote by author and journalist Arianna Huffington that expresses this concept perfectly is: "Failure is not the opposite of success; it's a part of success." Failing helps you learn, ultimately bringing you *closer* to success. You learn more about what you're trying to achieve, your capabilities, and what you need to do or improve in order to reach your goals. What's more empowering than embracing this?

Many people who fear failure are bona fide perfectionists. If this sounds like you, one of the best pieces of advice for embracing failure is to shift your mindset about your approach to your goal. Instead of striving for perfection every step of the way, try viewing what you're working on as an experiment. There is no such thing as perfection when you're experimenting with something! Sure, you can achieve success in your experiment, but nothing is perfect. Each experiment is conducted with the intention to learn from the result—both good and bad.

You're probably thinking, "But failing is *such* a big deal. How can I possibly feel confident when my fear of failing is so strong?" You're right. It's not easy to stay confident when you experience failure! Even those who are able to brush off certain setbacks still deal with doubt sometimes when something doesn't go the way they hoped. Even if you feel like you've completely made a 180-degree turn and embrace failure all of the time, it wouldn't be true. You're human, so remember that you will have highs and lows along the way.

Start with one day at a time. During each new day learn from your experiences, practice embracing the setbacks, and celebrate the wins. The more you enjoy the experiments, the more confident and awesome you'll feel about what you can accomplish.

BUILD POSITIVE RESILIENCE

The truth is, you'll experience ups, downs, and everything in between in every part of your life. In order to stay strong and continue to believe in yourself during those downs, you'll need to build a strong sense of positivity that helps you bounce back after a difficult situation.

While it may seem difficult, especially if you tend to focus on the negative, something that can help is to simply "Fake it 'til you make it." Put on a smile even when you don't feel like smiling. Act confident and strong in those moments when you don't feel confident or strong. It may feel awkward at first. You may feel like a fraud, trying to show everyone you're strong and confident in your abilities, but the more you practice, the more you'll start to actually *feel* it. It's kind of like affirmations or a self-fulfilling prophecy: you subconsciously begin to believe what you're projecting, and you fulfill those beliefs.

Another key part of building positive resilience is suspending your victim mentality. Through this mentality, you view yourself as a victim who has absolutely no control over your circumstances or how you react to them. You blame others and don't take responsibility for yourself. Even if you feel like you don't have this mentality, you'd be surprised by how easily it can creep in during those tough situations where it may be more challenging to accept responsibility for something. You *need* to get rid of this habit when you find yourself in this kind of mindset! It's a complete game changer for your self-confidence. Once you remove the victim mentality, you start to feel more in control over what you can or can't do, and how you react to both good and bad situations.

For example, say you're experiencing a day where the world seems to be against you. You wake up late for work, your dog eats your favorite shoes, there is an accident on the freeway so you end up stuck in traffic, and your presentation for your boss somehow didn't save when you finished it last night. Pretty rough, right? Well, if you practice a victimized mindset, you'll think that absolutely everything was out of your control and there's nothing you can do to make it better. Your job is ruined, your boss probably hates you, and there's no way you're getting the promotion you've been working toward all year. Why even bother trying, right?

Wrong.

While some of these situations were indeed out of your control (it's not your fault that someone got into an accident on the freeway when you were already running late), you don't need to react to these events in a way that makes you feel helpless. Instead you can tell yourself, "Okay, this isn't ideal, but I'm going continue to do the best I can to turn this around." For starters, you can figure out what caused you to run late in the morning and make changes for the next morning. Do you need to go to bed earlier to feel more well rested? Is your alarm loud enough? Do you need to make your lunch or pick your outfit the night before? You can also make a plan for rectifying your presentation issues. Communicate with your boss about the technical issues you're having and how those may be fixed. Offer solutions, not excuses. The key to taking control of the day is through staying proactive.

Remember that releasing the victim mindset and adapting a proactive mentality isn't something that's achieved overnight. It takes practice and constant awareness. The activities in this book will help you develop this more optimistic and proactive mindset. Try your best to remain consistent and use these tools to build that positive resilience, and you'll feel more awesome than ever before!

SURROUND YOURSELF WITH POSITIVE PEOPLE

Something you must learn is how incredibly important and unselfish it is to cut ties with toxic relationships. Whether platonic, romantic, or anywhere in between, your relationships should lift you up, not tear you down. Plus, how on earth are you going to build your self-confidence if you allow others to pull you in the other direction?

Sometimes toxic relationships are obvious, sometimes they are subtle. You might not even realize that you're experiencing a negative relationship. Some signs of these relationships include major highs and anxiety-ridden lows, consistently having personal boundaries crossed, and feeling like you're putting much more effort and care into the relationship than the other person. If any of this sounds familiar, it's time to consider if the relationship is actually a healthy one. The other person in the relationship might not have malicious intent. Sometimes two people simply aren't meant to be in a relationship at certain levels, and that's okay. A perfect anonymous quote that describes the kinds of relationships you deserve is, "Stick to the people who pull the magic out of you, not the madness." At the end of the day, if you notice you feel drained after each interaction with a certain person and they are unable or unwilling to fulfill your needs, it's time to put your mental health first.

It may not be easy. In fact, cutting negative people out of your life is probably one of the hardest things you will do for yourself. However, doing so is absolutely worth it. Whoever you're distancing yourself from may try to bring you back by saying he or she can change. At this point you've given enough chances, and know that this is who that person is. The odds of him or her changing are extremely slim. That person has had a chance. It's time to put *you* first. You are *not* selfish for making yourself a priority and putting your mental health and happiness above something that's not serving you.

If you distance yourself and the person never reaches out, then you know exactly how he or she felt about the relationship in the first place. Is that person truly a friend if he or she doesn't care enough to try? Life is too short to spend time on negative people. There are plenty of positive, beautiful people just waiting to help you feel even more awesome!

KEEP LEARNING AND GROWING

No one's perfect. Even your biggest role model isn't perfect. In fact, there is not a single person in this world who can't grow and improve in some way in his or her life. This shouldn't discourage you in any way, but help you understand that you're not alone in this journey. The more you grow and improve, the more confident and awesome you'll feel about yourself.

There are so many ways you can seek out self-improvement and growth. Some examples include:

▶ Books
▶ Blogs
▶ Podcasts
▶ Online courses
▶ Community classes

If you're new to the self-help realm, it can be difficult to figure out exactly where to start and what to focus on. Good news, though: you bought this book! You're already ahead of the game: you've started your personal growth journey!

Something to keep in mind about self-help and personal development is that there really isn't an "end goal." You're never officially "done" growing. Don't let this intimidate you! This just means that there are always opportunities to learn throughout your wonderful life. Each lesson you learn helps build the layers of who you are and what you can accomplish.

At some point during your journey, you'll find yourself in the "I don't have anywhere to grow" trap. You will have overcome personal struggles, landed a solid job you enjoy, and found amazing people who support you along the way. You'll feel like you've made it—what else is there for you to work on? You don't need personal development anymore. Clearly you have everything figured out. Boy, is this wrong. Even when you achieve your most challenging goals, you'll eventually start feeling stuck and unfulfilled. What you don't realize is that there are so many ways you can continue growing to avoid feeling stuck. You can invest more time in a hobby you love, start learning something new, create a consistent exercise routine and schedule, or look into planning and saving for brand-new travel experiences.

Life doesn't just stop once you hit your goals. Allowing yourself to plateau is simply accepting that you can't do anything else. Honestly, this sounds pretty boring. Wouldn't you rather continue to learn and grow? The journey is the most exciting place to be: it's where you experience the most fulfilling and enriching times in your life. When you reach your goal, celebrate, but don't stop there! You are capable of so much more. Imagine how much more confident you'll feel each time you learn more about yourself and what you can accomplish.

You are one beautiful, amazing human being, even if you don't believe it yet. It's time to realize just how *awesome* you truly are! Are you ready? Let's get started!

PART 2

ACTIVITIES

WRITE OUT YOUR EPIC LIFE

Each day is a chance for a wonderful, exciting adventure. Viewing each day as this special opportunity is a simple way to feel awesome about your life and what you're doing every day. In the following book, write out the events of your day today as though it is an epic novel. Don't leave any detail out, no matter how small! Every event is a key part of your amazing journey.

Once Upon A Time

Extinguish the Negativity

On a separate piece of paper, write down all of your insecurities, fears, worries—anything negative that you feel about yourself and your life. Now take the page and physically destroy it: burn it, drown it, bury it, rip it to shreds—anything you desire in order to get rid of it forever. You don't need that negativity in your life anymore. It's time to focus on what's awesome about you!

BLOCK OUT THE NOISE

People often find themselves attempting to live up to someone else's expectations—whether it's trying to land a certain kind of job, participate in certain hobbies or sports, or choose a certain "profitable" major. In order to feel awesome and find true happiness, you'll need to stop listening to those outside voices and pay attention to what's on the inside. Fill in the speech bubbles with all of the pressures and expectations that others push onto your life, whatever you feel like you're supposed to do, but don't actually want. Get them all out of your system.

DRAW YOUR
AWESOME PATH

It doesn't matter if you feel stuck where you are in life right now, or feel like you haven't done everything you should have by now. You are exactly where you are supposed to be, and are destined for greatness in the future—see for yourself!

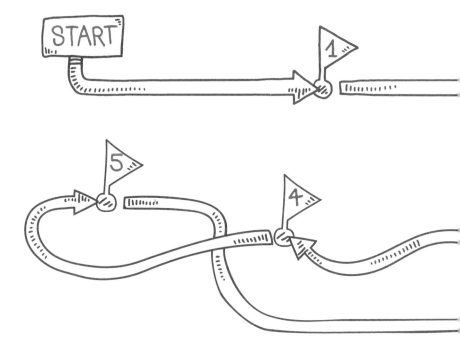

Write or draw out all of the milestones in your life from past to present on the road map provided here. These milestones can include highs, lows, and everything in between. You can include moments that made you grow, smile, laugh, cry...it's your beautiful life on which to reminisce. Once you get to the "You Are Here!" indicator, write exactly how you feel in this moment after looking back. Then fill in the space after the "X" with all of your dreams and goals for the future.

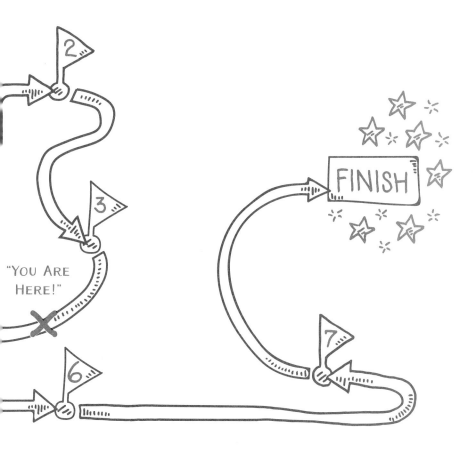

FOLLOW YOUR HEART

Fill in the heart with what you want in your life. What are some of your wildest, craziest dreams? No matter how big or small, include everything that can and will bring happiness into your life. These are the goals you should follow. They're yours, and they are awesome.

TAKE BABY STEPS

As you start moving forward in your self-confidence journey, you may find yourself stepping on the gas a bit too much, taking on every exercise and piece of advice until you quickly become overwhelmed. Instead, it's best to start with a few simple, clear steps to get the hang of your new, exciting adventure.

In the following space, write down three goals you'd like to achieve in your journey to feeling awesome. Then, write down one simple action that you can take right now toward each goal. Focus on completing these actions before doing anything else, and continue to move one step at a time through your self-confidence journey!

GOALS .... FIRST STEPS ....

1.

2.

3.

REDISCOVER YOUR BEAUTY

It can be easy to forget that who you are right now is just as beautiful and awesome as who you're striving to be. In the space provided, draw a picture of your present self, and include any photos or words to describe all of the parts of you that make you beautiful and awesome in this moment.

Try a Little Self-Care

Self-care is an essential part of your self-confidence journey. Here are a few simple ways to take care of yourself:

DRINK WATER

TAKE A NAP

GO FOR A WALK

SMILE

TAKE A HOT SHOWER OR BATH

CUDDLE WITH A PET

COLOR YOUR EMOTIONS

Draw how you've been feeling lately. Use colors to fully express the emotions you've experienced. For example, if you've been angry you can use red, and if you've been happy you can use yellow.

After, think about why you've been feeling these ways. Are there external factors causing these emotions? Or something inside sparking these negative or positive feelings? Becoming mindful of your emotions and their causes is an important first step toward gaining a better understanding of who you are.

THROW A PARTY

Celebrating small victories is just as important as celebrating your major accomplishments. Plan out a party for these small victories. Who is invited? What are the little wins that you're celebrating? How are you going to celebrate them? You can even set a theme if you want to!

GUESTS
....

SMALL
VICTORIES
....

ACTIVITIES
....

TURN TO YOUR
INNER CIRCLE

-If you're unsure about what makes you shine like the beautiful and awesome human you are, survey close people in your life about what positive traits and talents they admire in you. These people can be friends, family members, or even coworkers or teachers.

Use the following template to survey these chosen individuals. Afterward, apply the prompts on the following page to take the next step toward feeling awesome about these beautiful parts of yourself!

POSITIVE FEATURES SURVEY

Circle the characteristics you feel best describe me:

HONEST	FUNNY	INSPIRING
LOYAL	AUTHENTIC	CULTURED
INTELLIGENT	FAIR	DETERMINED
DOWN-TO-EARTH	BRAVE	IMAGINATIVE
CREATIVE	GENEROUS	ORGANIZED
PASSIONATE	LOVING	CALM
RESPONSIBLE	OPTIMISTIC	ROMANTIC
HUMBLE	HARDWORKING	
COMPASSIONATE	ADVENTUROUS	

Please describe me in a brief sentence.

....

....

....

NOW, REVIEW THESE RESPONSES AND ANSWER THE FOLLOWING QUESTIONS.

....

What were the most common characteristics and traits that described you?

....

Are any of the responses surprising to you?

....

Do you agree or disagree with these responses?
Why do you agree or disagree with them?

....

What are some ways you can celebrate and focus on these awesome characteristics?

REMEMBER YOUR STRENGTH

"Success is not final, failure is not fatal: it is the courage to continue that counts."

WINSTON CHURCHILL, British prime minister and writer

Failure is terrifying, but it's a part of life. Think about a time that you failed. How did you pull through? What helped you move forward? Write about it here. Next time you fail, remind yourself that it will be okay. You will make it through.

REFRESH YOUR WARDROBE

"Your appearance is your expression to others about who you are and what you stand for. The way you look reflects your self-image, attitude, confidence, and state of mind."

NATALIE JOBITY, author and consultant

What you wear and how you present yourself can have a direct correlation to how you feel about yourself. Why waste your time (and space in your closet) with clothes that don't help you feel like a million bucks?

Go through your closet and take out each piece of clothing that doesn't help you feel awesome. Do you really need that ratty T-shirt from your high school summer camp? Probably not. Donate it! Then, create outfits from each piece that does boost your confidence, and start filling the newfound extra space in your closet with similar types of clothes.

MOVE FORWARD

Take some time to meditate about your past failures. Are any of these failures still haunting you? Why do you think you're holding on to these experiences? Use the following space to reflect, then move onto the next page for further guidance.

What steps can you take to finally put them in the past? In order to truly feel confident in yourself, you'll need to let go of both past and any future failures you have and will experience in your life.

COMBAT NEGATIVE THOUGHTS

It's easy to get trapped in a negative belief about yourself—even if it's presented as a joke. Often, people use self-deprecating humor to lighten the mood (seeing a picture of dumpster on fire and saying, "Wow, look, a photo of my life!"), but even making these types of comments subconsciously reinforces negative beliefs about yourself. Take charge of your thoughts and start breaking these bad habits to finally feel awesome!

Write down each negative thought about yourself in the left column on the next page. In the right column, combat those thoughts with positive truths. For example, if you consistently think, "I'm a failure," combat this with an achievement you've made—no matter how big or small!

NEGATIVE THOUGHT

. . . .

FIGHT BACK!

. . . .

SAY **Goodbye** TO

YOUR WORRIES

Those who are self-confident rarely care about what other people think about them. It's time you nix these worries too! In the left column here, write down all of your fears about what other people might think of you. Are you scared that they judge your appearance? Your hobbies? Your interests in music? Next, write the following response to every fear in the right column: it doesn't matter.

WORRY

TRUTH

DISCOVER YOUR DREAMS

It's easy to back down from fear of failing, instead choosing a sure thing. However, if you really want to feel awesome, you're going to need to break out of this comfort zone and go after what you want. But first things first: what exactly do you want? Use the left column to explore this question, then use the right column to brainstorm just how to make it happen.

WHAT DO I WANT?	WHAT WILL I DO TO GET IT?
....	....

BUILD YOUR STRENGTHS

Write down your top five strengths. Then pick one of these talents and create an action plan on the following page to improve it even more. Ideas for refining your talent include signing up for an in-person or online class, practicing for ten minutes each day, or reading a book to learn more.

MY TALENTS:

....

....

....

....

....

....

....

....

....

....

....

....

....

....

CHOSEN TALENT:

....
....
....

HOW I WILL BECOME AN EXPERT:

....
....
....
....
....
....
....
....
....
....
....
....

BEGIN
THE DAY
WITH
GRATITUDE

Start each day by stating something you're truly grateful for. Is there someone in your life who helps you feel awesome? Did you get to experience a delicious food this week? Were you able to take time yesterday to watch a show or movie that you love? Try to think of something new every day! Starting the day with positivity will set you up for an awesome day.

TRANSFORM YOUR WEAKNESSES

When you don't feel confident, you often focus on your weaknesses. It's time to view those weaknesses as opportunities to grow!

1. Label each pot with a weakness.

2. Fill the watering cans with ways you can help those weaknesses grow into strengths.

3. Draw a flower (or a favorite plant) growing out of each pot. Use the blank tags to label each of these plants with a goal.

EXPLORE NEW ACTIVITIES

What are some new hobbies you've always wanted to try? Write them down, and then write ways you can develop them into new skills! Trying new things and gaining new skills are fantastic ways to start feeling good about yourself and what you can do!

HOBBIES

....

NEXT STEPS

....

1.

2.

3.

4.

5.

BE *Thankful*

Having a bad day? Use the following space to write down the three things you are thankful for right now. Don't think—just answer with the first things that pop into your head! Having the evidence on paper makes it easier to reframe your current mindset in a more positive way, so you can recognize just how awesome your life is!

1. ....

2. ....

3. ....

FORGIVE YOURSELF

It's time to stop beating yourself up about past mistakes. On the following page, write a letter to your past self about these mistakes. End the letter with, "I forgive you."

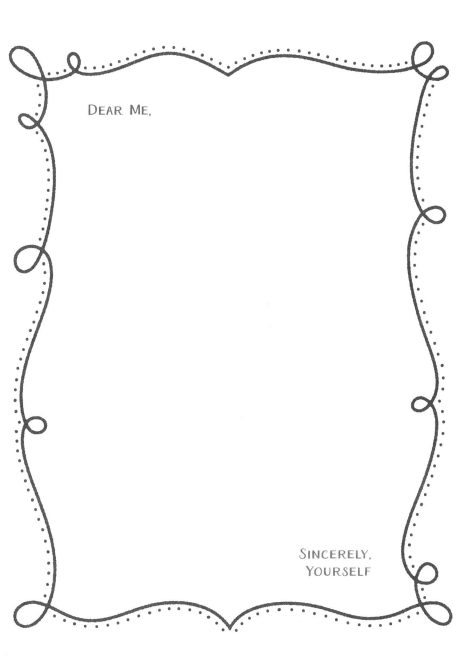

DEAR ME,

SINCERELY,
YOURSELF

GET READY

Prepare yourself for your awesome adventure ahead! Write down any possible obstacles to your goals. After, create a to-do list on the next page with ways to prepare for those potential twists and turns in your life's journey!

POTENTIAL CHALLENGES.

1.

2.

3.

4.

5.

MY TO-DOS.

☐ ....
☐ ....
☐ ....
☐ ....
☐ ....
☐ ....
☐ ....
☐ ....
☐ ....
☐ ....
☐ ....
☐ ....
☐ ....
☐ ....
☐ ....
☐ ....
☐ ....
☐ ....
☐ ....
☐ ....
☐ ....

SEEK INSPIRATION

What is one quote that inspires you? Go online and find one that strikes a chord in your heart. Then, write this quote on sticky notes and place the notes around your house—your bathroom mirror, bedroom door, and even the rearview mirror in your car! You can also use the space here to jot down your quote and brainstorm places to put it.

Train Your Brain

Affirmations are a wonderful tool for when you need a little reminder of how awesome you are. Next time you're struggling to feel confident about yourself, whether it's about your appearance, talents, or current situation, recite one (or all) of the following affirmations with strength and certainty—even if you don't actually feel it:

▶ I COMPLETELY BELIEVE IN MYSELF.

▶ I AM STRONG.

▶ I AM MORE THAN ENOUGH.

▶ I TRUST MYSELF.

▶ I AM CAPABLE OF AWESOME THINGS.

▶ I AM BEAUTIFUL.

▶ I HAVE EVERYTHING I NEED TO ACCOMPLISH EVERYTHING I WANT.

▶ I. AM. *AWESOME.*

The more you recite these affirmations, the more you'll start to believe in what you're saying.

STEP OUTSIDE OF YOUR COMFORT ZONE

One way to start building more self-confidence is by stepping outside of your comfort zone through new experiences. When was the last time you tried something new? Write about it in the following space. How did you feel in the moment? How did it feel after you were done? Start practicing saying yes to new experiences and opportunities. You never know what you will end up enjoying, and you may even pick up a new skill or passion along the way!

MAKE TIME FOR YOU

Do you struggle to make time for yourself? It's easy to become so busy with all of your responsibilities and social obligations that you forget to put yourself first. Use the following space to write a "Me Day" action plan for the next time you need to make yourself a priority. Include anything that helps you feel recharged, happy, and ready to take on the world.

REEXAMINE CRITICISM

Criticism from others, whether constructive or not, has the potential to either make or break how you feel about yourself. It is important to learn how to positively embrace or release criticism, instead of taking it personally. This takes time and practice, but through your diligence, you'll slowly grow more confident.

Beyond growing thicker skin, you can also use criticism to understand something you can improve about yourself. One way to do this is by rewriting the tough words in a more constructive format that allows you to see the true intent. If the intent was primarily positive, then rewriting this feedback will help you understand what you need to work on. If the criticism was simply rude, you can then let it go.

On the next page, interpret the following criticisms in your own words and determine if they are constructive or don't deserve your attention.

⏵⏵ (Example)

CRITICISM: "Your presentation was really informative. However, I recommend speaking a little slower in the future to ensure the audience embraces all of your important points."

INTERPRETATION: "I had great content and research to share in my presentation, but the audience may not have been able to grasp all of my concepts because I was speaking too quickly."

Was this constructive? Yes.

The example had good intentions and was constructive. Now you know an area of public speaking you can improve on in order to be a stronger presenter in the future.

Now it's your turn!

CRITICISM: "While I do appreciate your enthusiasm, interrupting me makes me feel like you aren't listening to what I have to say."

INTERPRETATION:
Was this constructive?

....

....

....

....

....

....

CRITICISM: "Your new haircut is a joke. How could you possibly think that was a good idea?"

INTERPRETATION:
Was this constructive?

....

....

....

....

....

....

LET GO OF TOXIC RELATIONSHIPS

In order to fully feel confident in yourself, you'll need to have a strong support system, filled with positive people who encourage you through all of the highs and lows in your life. To achieve this solid foundation of loved ones, you'll need to weed out any negative relationships. Use the following steps to take a closer look at the people in your life and see if you need to start taking steps toward letting a negative relationship go.

1. In the space provided, write the names of people you inter- act with on a regular basis. These include friends, coworkers, and family.

....

....

....

2. Go through the names and think about the relationship you have with each person. Is the relationship more positive than negative? How does that person make you feel about yourself?

3. Identify the people you believe need to be removed from your life in order for you to move forward and feel self-confident.

4. Take action to change your relationships with those toxic people. Some ways to do this include:
   ▶ Slowly talking to them and seeing them less. You can be cordial, but not engaging.
   ▶ Being upfront and honest about how you feel. Be fair, but explain your situation and how you feel your relationship with them affects you.
   ▶ Removing or blocking them on social media.

ACKNOWLEDGE THE GOOD

*"Every day may not be good,
but there is good in every day."*

UNKNOWN

What are the good things that happened in your life today?
Write these things down in the space provided as a reminder
that even in your lowest moments, there is still something
beautiful and truly awesome about being alive.

PLAN A TRIP

What are some places in this world that you'd love to visit? Color in the map and label your dream destinations! Traveling is an excellent way to build self-esteem, create new relationships, and grow!

CREATE A POSITIVITY LIST

Even though positive thinking can be difficult (negative thoughts are often easier, after all!), incorporate the following activity into your daily routine.

1. Choose a way to create a list that you can keep with you throughout the day. This can be through notes in your phone, a notebook that you carry around, a Post-it you keep in your pocket, a napkin you find in your car—anything!

2. Throughout your day, take note of anything and everything positive around you. It can be a cute dog during your commute to work, a pretty flower outside your window, or the deep blue sky and puffy clouds of a beautiful day. No matter how big or small they may be, write down anything that brings you joy.

3. At the end of the day, review your list and reflect on all of the good things you experienced. Practice graciousness in these beautiful moments and take pride in the fact that you made the effort to engage in this act of positive mindfulness.

GIVE YOURSELF A HAND
(AND A TROPHY)

You are filled with beautiful qualities and unique talents.
Take pride in who you are and what you do! Fill in the trophy
with drawings or words describing what you're proud of about
yourself. This can include accomplishments and talents. Don't
hold back!

EXPLORE EMOTION

1. Place a checkmark next to the emotions you think you need to feel in order to be more confident in yourself.

HAPPINESS   KINDNESS   FEAR

BOREDOM

DISAPPOINTMENT   LONELINESS

EXCITEMENT   IRRITATION   RELIEF

SHAME

TRUST   LOVE

DISGUST   CONTENTMENT

PRIDE

ENVY   HOPE   EXHAUSTION

ANTICIPATION

ANXIETY   SURPRISE   SADNESS

2. Now, circle the emotions you've actually experienced lately. Guess what! Everyone, even those who seem so self-confident, has experienced the emotions you circled. It's because they're human, just like you. And emotions (good and bad) are part of experiencing life to the fullest.

SQUASH
THOSE DOUBTS

What is something about yourself that
you're feeling rather doubtful about
lately? Spend today telling yourself you
are exactly the opposite. For example,
if you're constantly thinking that you
aren't smart enough for your job, spend
the day thinking, "I am brilliant and
excellent at my work." See how you feel
at the end of the day, then try it
again the following day. Keep going each
day, then see how you feel at the end of
the week. Take note of any differences
in what you were able to accomplish. You
will surprise yourself!

PRACTICE GOOD POSTURE

Here's a simple change to give yourself a quick and immediate confidence boost: stand up straight! Studies show that good posture creates a subconscious mental shift. Not only will others see you as a more confident individual; it will also improve the way you view yourself.

Be Kind

You'd be amazed by how much simple, random acts of kindness can uplift your spirit and help you feel fantastic. Start implementing little acts of kindness throughout the week, and see how it not only makes you feel, but also how it influences the people you're helping. Some ideas for random acts of kindness include:

- ▶ Paying for the person behind you in the coffee shop line. Oftentimes this will even trigger that person to follow suit and start a "pay it forward" chain!
- ▶ Opening the door for someone next time you're walking into or out of a building.
- ▶ Giving someone extra space to merge into your lane on the freeway.
- ▶ Leaving money in a vending machine for the next person who wants a snack.
- ▶ Letting someone go in front of you in a line.
- ▶ Complimenting a stranger.
- ▶ Smiling!

VOLUNTEER

Take random acts of kindness a step further by giving back to your community. Your help will make a difference for those in need, and help you feel capable of great things. Give some of the following volunteer ideas a try:

DONATE SOME OF YOUR CLOTHES AND BLANKETS TO A LOCAL SHELTER.

SIGN UP TO VOLUNTEER AT AN ANIMAL SHELTER.

PICK UP TRASH ALONG THE STREET OR AT A LOCAL PARK.

BAKE COOKIES FOR A RETIREMENT HOME.

There's so much you can do to give back to your community. Check out online community postings, church bulletin boards, and the local paper to see what catches your eye—you never know what you'll find available nearby!

DO IT

What's one thing that you've always been scared of doing? Are you afraid of saying hi to a stranger, making a doctor's appointment, or giving a presentation? Write this fear in the space provided.

NOW GO DO IT!

LEARN FROM YOUR PAST

Recall a time when you felt terrified, but decided to face your fears and go for it anyway. What happened? How did you feel before, during, and after the experience?

FEAR	BEFORE	DURING	AFTER

Next time you're afraid, reflect back on this moment and remember how you were able to get through it. It may be terrifying, but you are truly awesome for facing your fears!

ESTABLISH YOUR VALUES

It's much easier to make decisions when you know what your personal values are. Do you know your values? What are they? Use this space to do a bit of soul-searching and discover what things are important to you.

CREATE A SELF-PORTRAIT

You may tend to worry about how others see you, but how do you see yourself? Draw an honest illustration of how you see yourself in the space provided here. Alternatively, describe you perspective in as much detail as you can.

Why do you see yourself this way? If this image or description doesn't make you happy, what are some ways to change it?

MOVE YOUR BODY

Having one of those days where you feel sluggish and unmotivated? Get up and move! Not sure how? You can try:

Dancing

Going for a walk

Swimming

Exploring a nearby hiking trail or path in a park

Jogging or running

Stretching or yoga

Finding a workout video online

Simply find something that gets your blood pumping and has you feelin' good!

What activities did you try to help you get out of your sluggish funk? Do you have any other ideas for fun ways to get up and move? Write them down!

MAKE A "COMFORT LIST"

Do you have a favorite song or quote that never fails to make you feel great, no matter what's happening in your life? Have you ever taken a moment to think about why these specific things make you feel so good? Well, now's your chance! Write your answers to each question in the provided space.

WHAT'S YOUR FAVORITE QUOTE? Why is this your favorite quote? Are there specific situations in your life that this quote has helped you endure, or does it simply bring a feeling of joy when you read it?

DO YOU HAVE A SONG OR SPECIFIC LYRIC that consistently helps you feel awesome? Why do you think it helps you feel this way? Is it the message, the beat, or the artist singing it?

IS THERE A BOOK THAT YOU'VE READ that has stuck with you in a positive way? What was it about, and why did it resonate with you?

WHAT MOVIE OR TV SHOW NEVER FAILS to put a smile on your face? What about this movie or show helps you feel good? Do you relate to any of the characters, or perhaps the story?

Whenever you're feeling down, refer to these resources as your "Comfort List." Any time you come across new quotes, songs, books, movies, or TV shows that help you feel awesome, add them to the list and keep them in mind for when you need an extra boost in feeling like your awesome self!

QUIT
PROCRASTINATING

Is there something you've been
procrastinating on lately? Have you wanted
to get back into a workout routine? Is
there a project at school or work that you
should have started already?
Or maybe you've been meaning to make plans
with someone close to you, but
never got around to it?
Go do it. Right now. Seriously, just do it.
You'll be glad you did.

GET ORGANIZED

When was the last time you cleaned your room, desk, or other personal space? Many people can't be productive or feel relaxed unless their space is clutter-free. So give it a try, and notice how it benefits your productivity and overall well-being.

PRACTICE
STRESS
MANAGEMENT

What are some ways that you currently manage
your stress? List them here.

If you're unsure how to manage your stress, or feel that the ways you try to manage stress aren't actually helping, here are some recommended techniques:

PRACTICE DEEP BREATHING. BREATHING OUT SLIGHTLY LONGER THAN YOU BREATHE IN WILL HELP CLEAR YOUR MIND.

DO A MEDITATION OR YOGA ROUTINE.

SCHEDULE REGULAR SHORT WALKS THROUGHOUT YOUR DAY.

LISTEN TO WHAT YOUR BODY IS CRAVING AND GIVE IT WHAT IT NEEDS.

TRACK YOUR ZZZs

Feeling good starts with simply getting enough sleep at night. While each person's needs may vary, experts recommend getting seven to nine hours of sleep every night. Keep track of how many hours you sleep each night with the following chart. Include how you felt during the next day. At the end of each week, notice any patterns with your sleep schedule and overall energy and behavior, and adjust to what you feel is best for your body.

WEEK ONE	HOURS SLEPT	HOW I FELT
MONDAY		
TUESDAY		
WEDNESDAY		
THURSDAY		
FRIDAY		
SATURDAY		
SUNDAY		

WEEK TWO	HOURS SLEPT	HOW I FELT
MONDAY		
TUESDAY		
WEDNESDAY		
THURSDAY		
FRIDAY		
SATURDAY		
SUNDAY		
WEEK THREE	HOURS SLEPT	HOW I FELT
MONDAY		
TUESDAY		
WEDNESDAY		
THURSDAY		
FRIDAY		
SATURDAY		
SUNDAY		

REMIND YOURSELF...

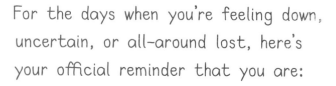

For the days when you're feeling down, uncertain, or all-around lost, here's your official reminder that you are:

BEAUTIFUL, AMAZING, TALENTED, WONDERFUL, INSIGHTFUL, FANTASTIC, STRONG, INCREDIBLE, INSPIRING, MAGICAL, EXCITING, EXCEPTIONAL, CAPABLE, EXCELLENT, AUTHENTIC, CHERISHED, TRUSTWORTHY, DAZZLING, ENCHANTING, FABULOUS, UNIQUE, SPECTACULAR, RADIANT, LOVELY, IRRESISTIBLE, EXTRAORDINARY,

and above all else:

YOU. ARE. AWESOME.

DRESS
THE PART

A big contributor to feeling awesome is how you put yourself together for the day. If you spend most of your days in sweatpants and ratty old T-shirts and don't shower for a week, you can't possibly feel confident and capable. Taking the extra time to make yourself look good, even through something as simple as showering and wearing presentable clothes, can make a world of difference.

For the next week, really make an extra effort to look your best, whether you have somewhere to go or not. At the end of the week, reflect on the difference it made in your attitude about yourself. You'll be surprised at just how much better you will feel each day compared to your sweats-and-ratty-T-shirt days!

CONSIDER
THE POSSIBILITIES

Comparing yourself to others is a trap. How on earth are you supposed to feel good about yourself if you're constantly comparing yourself negatively to others? Additionally, most of the time people only share the good things happening in their lives, not the bad.

Log on to whichever social media account you use most and find a photo or status update about an exciting life event. At first glance, how does it make you feel? What are your first thoughts when you see this?

....

....

....

....

Next, write down all of the possible things that could also be occurring behind the scenes of this photo or update. Maybe he or she had an argument with a friend before booking this vacation. Maybe the newlywed couple had budgeting problems before buying this house.

....

....

....

....

Now take a look at one of your photos or status updates. Write about the truth behind this exciting post you shared on social media. Whether good or bad, what truly happened leading up to that moment?

....

....

....

....

....

....

....

....

....

....

....

....

....

....

The next time you're negatively comparing yourself to someone else on social media, remember this activity. There's always a bigger picture behind the post. Never forget that.

FUEL YOUR BODY

While a main part of self-confidence is how you feel mentally, it also involves how you feel physically. A huge component of feeling good is what you're feeding your body. No matter your size or shape, certain foods can have a positive or negative effect on your overall well-being and how you feel about yourself. For the next week, use the chart on the following page to keep track of the types of foods you're putting in your body and how you feel at the end of the day. This isn't about counting calories or carbs, but noticing how you feel when you eat certain types of foods. Food should be fuel to help you feel better, not worse.

Please do *not* consider this as a way to feel guilty about your eating habits. If you feel good when you have a sweet treat every once in a while, then that's great! You deserve it! Use this chart as a step toward creating more mind-ful habits that help you be the best version of yourself.

	SUNDAY	SATURDAY	FRIDAY	THURSDAY	WEDNESDAY	TUESDAY	MONDAY
BREAKFAST							
LUNCH							
DINNER							
SNACKS							
HOW I FEEL							

MEDITATE

Go online and find a meditation practice to try today.
Meditation can help you ease anxious thoughts and
negativity, and also give you an opportunity to reflect on
both your current skills and ways that you can improve
so you feel even more awesome. After you try the
meditation exercise, use the space here to write about
your experience. What did it reveal? How do you feel?

ACCEPT YOUR AWARD

Think back to a time when you accomplished something amazing. This can be big or small, but should be something that made you feel awesome about yourself. Write a thank-you speech in the space provided as if you are accepting an award for your accomplishment. When you're done, read the speech out loud as a reminder of how awesome you truly are!

MAKE A
MOOD-BOOSTING
PLAYLIST

Create a playlist of your all-time favorite feel-good
songs on the following page. Next time you're feeling
down and need a quick mood boost or inspiration for the
day, listen and dance along to this playlist! If you need
some ideas for songs to add to this awesome list, check
out the empowering songs provided in the Appendix of
this book!

MY ABSOLUTE
FAVORITE SONGS

LOOK TO
YOUR ROLE MODELS

Who are some of your role models? Reflecting on who you look up to and aspire to be like helps you discover what you value in life. Write down the role models in your life in the left-hand column provided. These can be people you know personally (family members, friends, teachers, etc.) and even popular figures (celebrities, historical icons, etc.). In the right-hand column, write down three to five positive traits that you admire in each of these people. What about them inspires you? In what ways do you wish you were more like them?

ROLE MODELS

POSITIVE TRAITS

Now write down your name in that left-hand column. What are some beautiful and admirable qualities you find in yourself? Explore this as if you were someone else observing and admiring you from afar. What values and traits about yourself inspire you? You can answer these questions here, and add those positive traits to the right-hand column.

While it's great to look to other people for inspiration as your role models, don't forget that you have wonderful qualities and talents yourself that inspire other people. Next time you're feeling a bit unsure about yourself, refer back to this chart and remind yourself of the reasons why you're awesome.

SPREAD THE *Love*

It's well known that encouraging other people is a great way to feel awesome while making a difference. Plus, you may be surprised to discover that your actions come back around in the best way. Compliment three people today. They can be close friends, family members, acquaintances, or complete strangers. Take the time to brighten their day, and notice how they respond and how you feel afterward.

TAP INTO YOUR INNER CHILD

What are some things that
made you smile as a child?
Revisit some of these activities
that you enjoyed when you were young.
They can be movies, hobbies, songs—anything!
Afterward, reflect in the space provided on what
you tried and how it made you feel. Discover what still
brings a smile to your face and makes you feel good!

DEFINE "AWESOME"

While there are dictionary definitions for terms relating to self-confidence, everyone has their own personal definitions for what each of these words mean to them. Read the official definitions from www.dictionary.com for the following words. Afterward, on the following page, write your own definitions for each of these terms. Notice the differences between the two definitions and why that may be. The more familiar you are with your own definitions and what you find important in each term, the more confident you'll feel when recognizing these things as they occur in your unique and awesome life!

••

SUCCESS ▶ The favorable or prosperous termination of attempts or endeavors; the accomplishment of one's goals.

FAILURE ▶ An act or instance of failing or proving unsuccessful; lack of success.

CONFIDENCE ▶ Full trust; belief in the powers, trustworthiness, or reliability of a person or thing.

SELF-ESTEEM ▶ A realistic respect for or favorable impression of oneself; self-respect.

DREAMS ▶ A succession of images, thoughts, or emotions passing through the mind during sleep.

PRODUCTIVITY ▶ The quality, state, or fact of being able to generate, create, enhance, or bring forth goods and services.

Now that you know the boring technical definitions for these important terms, it's your turn: how would you personally define each of these words? How can you make them special in order to help you discover what each of these means to you throughout your self-confidence journey?

••

SUCCESS ▶

FAILURE ▶

CONFIDENCE ▶

SELF-ESTEEM ▶

DREAMS ▶

PRODUCTIVITY ▶

LOOK AT YOURSELF

One of the hardest things to do when you're feeling self-doubt is to look in a mirror. Your challenge today is to spend five full minutes looking in a mirror. No distractions, no interruptions. Pay attention to your thought patterns and challenge any negative feelings with positive and uplifting self-compliments. You're beautiful and awesome. Toss out any thoughts that say otherwise.

RELEASE WHAT
ISN'T IN YOUR CONTROL

When life starts pulling you in a million different directions, it can be tempting to grab on to every single thing and try to control it as much as possible. However, attempting this leads to burnout and feeling like a failure. Sound familiar?

The key is to realize what you can and cannot control. Once you do, you can let go of so much, shift your mindset, and tackle all of life's crazy responsibilities with confidence. When you find yourself feeling overwhelmed and as though your life is spiraling out of control, refer to the following lists and focus on what you can control, while letting go of what's out of your hands. Keep in mind that these aren't comprehensive lists, but are here to help you decide what *you* should focus on and where *you* should channel your energy when life gets crazy.

THINGS YOU CAN CONTROL:

- ▶ Your priorities
- ▶ How you react to situations
- ▶ How you express your emotions
- ▶ How you spend your time
- ▶ The effort you put into something
- ▶ Who you spend time with
- ▶ How you treat others
- ▶ What you eat and drink
- ▶ What you say

THINGS YOU CAN'T CONTROL:

- ▶ Others' opinions
- ▶ Others' actions
- ▶ Others' expectations
- ▶ The weather
- ▶ Traffic
- ▶ The long line at the grocery store
- ▶ Gas prices
- ▶ The future
- ▶ Cats

REFLECT ON
YOUR PROGRESS

While you're in the thick of following your dreams (or trying to figure out what they are), you may feel at times like you haven't made much progress. However, you'd be surprised to see just how much you've progressed—even over the span of one year!

Think back to where and how you were one year ago. What did you do during the typical day? What were you trying to accomplish? Who did you spend time with? If you need help remembering that far back, refer to social media, personal photos, or friends and family members.

Now, write down how much you've accomplished since then and how much has changed. No matter how big or small the changes, reflect on your progress.

TIP: Make this a yearly activity! At the same time every year, look back at your previous reflection and record how much you've changed since then. It's hard to not feel great about yourself when you realize just how far you've come!

BE
YOUR OWN
BEST FRIEND

When life gets overwhelming or you find yourself experiencing a crushing failure, it's easy to be hard on yourself, telling yourself that you're terrible or worthless. You absolutely need to break this cycle and be kind to yourself.

THINK: How would you speak to your best friend if he or she was in the same situation? Would you be as harsh? Probably not. Next time you find yourself in a tough situation, pay attention to what you're telling yourself. If you catch yourself giving criticisms and harsh words, act as if you're talking to a friend. Write a letter to yourself if you have to! Whatever helps you start treating yourself with more kindness.

MAKE IT A "DONE" LIST ✓

Swamped with an endless list of to-dos and feeling like you can't make any progress? It's easy to forget what you've accomplished when the list never seems to finish. At the end of your day, instead of writing another to-do list for the following day, start compiling a "Completed" list. List everything you were able to accomplish that day, whether it was running an errand, exercising, or working on a project. Notice how much better it feels to remind yourself of the awesome things you have done that day, rather than reminding yourself of the things that you haven't done.

CREATE YOUR
LIFE MOTTO

Making a life motto for yourself is a great way to narrow down your values, declare what kind of person you want to be, and continuously remind yourself of what you're striving for in life. However, creating one of these can be daunting, so we've made it a bit more fun with a fill-in-the-blank activity!

Fill in the different word types with corresponding terms that you'd like in your life motto. The only rule is to keep everything positive!

Adjective 1: _____ Adjective 2: _____

Adjective 3: _____ Noun 1: _____

Value 1: _____ Trait 1: _____

Verb 1: _____ Adjective 4: _____

Trait 2: _____ Trait 3: _____

Person You Love 1: _____

Verb 2: _____ Activity 1: _____

Verb 3: _____ Adverb 1: _____

Verb 4: _____ Activity 2: _____ ing

I am _____ , _____ , and _____ .
           (adjective 1)   (adjective 2)   (adjective 3)

I care about _____ , value _____ , and
                     (noun 1)   (value 1)

exemplify _____ .
                  (trait 1)

My purpose is to _____ . I strive to be a(n)
                          (verb 1)

_____ version of myself every day.
 (adjective 4)

The people I value are _____ , and I always admire the
                               (trait 2)

_____ displayed every day by _____ .
  (trait 3)   (person you love 1)

I learn best by _____ and love to _____ .
                       (verb 2)   (activity 1)

If things don't work out as planned, I will _____
                                                        (verb 3)

_____ instead of groveling and dwelling on what
  (adverb 1)

went differently.

I feel like the best version of myself when I _____ ,
                                                        (verb 4)

as well as when I spend time _____ .
                                     (activity 2)

TA-DA! You've officially created your first life motto! That
wasn't so difficult, was it?

OWN YOUR MISTAKES

In order to feel confident about yourself, you can't let the chance of being wrong keep you from speaking up. Taking chances includes the risk of failure, but that's all a part of the experience! Do you remember a time when you were wrong about something? What happened? What did you learn and how did you move forward from it? You can ponder these questions in the space provided.

SHARPEN YOUR SKILLS

Everyone feels awesome when they're good at something. What are some things that you're good at? What can you do to become even better at these things? For example, do you have a knack for drawing? Some ways you can improve this skill include searching for instructional videos online, finding free or low-cost courses in your area, or seeking out a mentor.

PROMOTE POSITIVITY WITH COLOR

Did you know that colors evoke certain feelings in people? For example, the color red promotes intense feelings like passion, while blue evokes calm and creativity.

WHAT'S YOUR FAVORITE COLOR?

Go online to discover what this color symbolizes, and what emotions it can trigger. Answer the following questions in the space here: does this new information surprise you? Or does it actually represent you and your emotions pretty accurately?

In the space provided, use a marker, colored pencil, or crayon in your favorite color to draw an entire scene that embodies this favorite color. You can doodle landscapes, people, faces—anything you want! Let your creativity and emotions flow. Then, reflect on how you feel when you express yourself with this color.

You can use colors to promote any feeling, so experiment with color in your décor, wardrobe, and even writing implements the next time you are in need of a bit of cheering up, inspiration, or relaxation!

REWARD YOUR ACCOMPLISHMENTS

One way to feel great while also accomplishing your goals is to set up a reward system. Use the left-hand column in the following chart to fill in your current short- and long-term goals. In the right-hand column, write down a reward you'll treat yourself to once you've completed each goal. Some ideas for rewards include having an ice cream cone, grabbing drinks with friends, or even taking a mini road trip for the weekend. Hint: long-term goals usually take more effort and time to complete, so make sure those rewards are a little more generous than the ones you dedicate to your short-term goals!

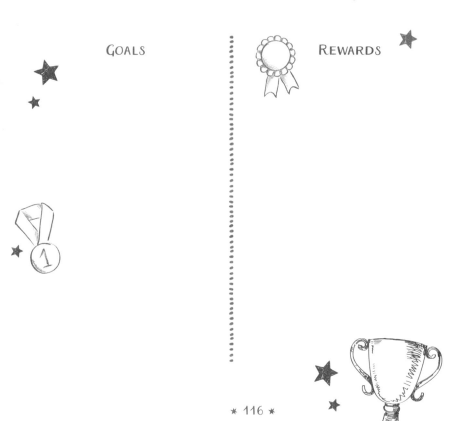

GOALS   REWARDS

TREAT YO'SELF

Need a quick pick-me-up for your self-esteem? Treat yourself to something that will lift your spirits! What's something small that will make your day just a little bit brighter? Get rid of any guilt and just go for it. You deserve it!

CHANGE YOUR POINT OF VIEW

When you're stuck in a rut, it's easy to feel like you have it worse than everyone else. However, you'd be surprised by how differently other people may see what you're experiencing. Think about your situation and how you're feeling. How might an outsider feel if they were in your shoes? What are some ways they might look at your situation differently? For example, if you're feeling stressed from struggling to find a job after college, a current college student might feel jealous that you're done with school, wishing to trade his or her exams and endless homework for your job search. Sometimes a shift in perspective is all you need to help you feel a bit more grateful for where you are in life. Use the space on the next page to write about your current struggles in someone else's point of view.

SPRUCE
THINGS UP

Feeling bored with your appearance?
Freshen things up with a new 'do, some
new pieces of clothing, or a slick pair of
new shoes! You'd be surprised by how much
a small change can help you feel like a
whole new awesome person!

PRACTICE VISUALIZATION

When you're getting ready for something terrifying, such as an interview or an important speech, a great way to build your confidence before facing this challenge is to practice visualizations. Studies show that visualizations help people achieve their goals and perform better overall because they know exactly what they need to do in order to succeed.

Next time you're preparing for something nerve-wracking, close your eyes for five to ten minutes and picture yourself kicking butt at what you're about to do. Don't just see yourself succeeding, *feel* how awesome it is to conquer this upcoming challenge. After, bring this feeling and newfound confidence into your task, and notice how much better you perform compared to if you had gone into it as a trembling ball of nerves.

REVISIT THE PAST

Is there something that terrifies you because of a past experience? For example, maybe you once went out on a limb to introduce yourself to someone new and it didn't go as planned, so now making the first move when meeting new people always reminds you of those awful feelings you had. Your mind remembers events through the feelings you experienced, but usually things in the past aren't as terrible as these feelings lead you to believe.

In the following space, recall an experience you went through that you associate with feelings of low self-esteem. Write down everything you remember, from the sequence of events to how you felt.

Now take some time to look at the same situation from a third party's objective point of view. Write this view in the space provided. If you're having trouble separating your emotions from the situation, see if there is a trusted friend or family member who was there and who can tell you what they remember.

••

Compare both versions and notice the similarities and differences. Was the experience just as traumatizing as you remember? The next time you approach a similar situation, how will you do things differently to feel more confident?

You can do anything. At the end of the day, remember that you are awesome, inspiring, and completely unstoppable. You've got this!

KEEP YOUR MIND ACTIVE

Personal growth is a powerful way to build your self-confidence. One of the best ways to grow is to stay curious: ask questions about things and keep an active and open mind through new experiences. When was the last time you learned something new? Did you ask questions, or did you simply accept everything you were taught?

Next time you experience something new, ask questions along the way. Activate your curiosity and create a new adventure out of whatever you're learning! You can also use the following space to keep track of what you've learned.

PHONE A FRIEND

Ask a close friend, partner, or family member why they think you're awesome. Write down their answer here, and the next time you need a little pick-me-up, refer to this page as a reminder of how awesome you are!

CHECK OUT THIS
IMPORTANT MESSAGE

Write down everything you define as "bad" happening in your life right now. Is anything annoying you? Are you experiencing continuous bad luck? What's frustrating you?

NOW SEE THE NEXT PAGE...

BREATHE

Feeling overwhelmed? It's hard to feel awesome when you're swamped with all of life's crazy demands. Take five minutes out of your day to do the following breathing activity. This activity will lower your stress and help you have a clearer vision of what exactly you can do to conquer your day.

1. While either sitting up straight or standing, place one hand on your stomach and the other hand on your chest.

2. Breathe deeply and slowly into your stomach. Make sure your chest doesn't move or expand, only your belly.

3. Breathe out, again taking your time and ensuring that only your stomach moves.

4. Continue these deep breaths five to ten times.

Notice how much calmer you feel. If you're having a hard time controlling your breathing, you can find a number of helpful smartphone apps.

OFFER
A HELPING
HAND

Helping other people is a fantastic way
to not only better someone else's life,
but also increase your own self-confidence
and sense of worth. Do something nice for
someone today. Afterward, write about your
experience in the space provided. What did
you do? How did you feel? How did the
other person feel?

BELIEVE IN YOU

*"Don't believe in magic—
the magic is in the believing!"*

UNKNOWN

WHAT DO YOU BELIEVE IN? These can be values, morals, people—whatever or whoever you truly believe in with all of your heart. Write these beliefs in the heart shown here.

MY BELIEFS

Did you include yourself in your list? If not, it's time to change that. Imagine how much magic you can create by taking the same level of belief you have for what you wrote down and channeling it into believing in yourself!

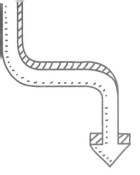

If you didn't include yourself in the heart on the previous page, why don't you believe in yourself? Take time and really dig deep—it'll be an important key to discovering what exactly you need to focus on in order to become the most confident version of yourself.

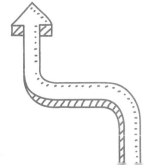

MAKE A PROMISE

In order to grow and create change in your life, you need to truly commit to this work. Keeping promises to yourself is incredibly important. After all, you don't like disappointing other people, so why should you be okay with continuously disappointing yourself?

Fill in the blanks on the next page with your name and signature to create an official personal commitment contract. Once signed, copy this page and post it where you can see it every day. Use it as a daily reminder of the promise you made to yourself, as well as a motivator in improving your confidence and life every day.

Date: _____

I, _____ , officially
promise to work each day toward believing
in myself and improving my self-confidence.

I understand that increasing my self-
esteem and self-development isn't an easy
task, but I'm ready to truly make a
difference and grow into the best version
of myself. I accept that it will take
determination, curiosity, and self-love to
accomplish my goals.

I'm ready for this. This is my time, and
starting today I will make a conscientious
effort to work on improving myself, not only
to benefit my life, but also to impact those
around me in a positive way.

Above all else, I know that this is the
start of my journey to finally, truly,
wholeheartedly believing that I am one of
a kind and completely awesome.

_____

Signature

UNDERSTAND THE IMPORTANCE OF HUMILITY

Once you start gaining traction in your journey to stronger self-confidence, you'll need to make sure you don't cross the delicate line into over-confidence. Staying humble is a valuable trait to have throughout your personal growth experience. Humility prevents you from judging others, helps you put less pressure on yourself, and encourages you to uplift others throughout any struggles they may be experiencing. If you're ever uncertain of whether your ego is a little swollen, see if you relate to any of these qualities:

1. You see yourself as superior to everyone else.

2. You won't listen to anyone's advice or suggestions.

3. You often interrupt or talk over other people.

4. Your relationships don't feel strong or valued.

5. You easily become defensive.

Do any of these sound familiar? If so, it's time to take a step back and revisit your values so you can move away from arrogance and toward graciousness and healthy levels of self-confidence.

REMEMBER THIS

Write this sentence down over and over again all over this page. Fill it up and repeat this exercise as many times as you need in order for the sentence to stick! (Running out of room? Write it down on any page of this book at any time!)

I am awesome.

RECOGNIZE WHAT YOU DESERVE

"Our deepest fear is not that we are inadequate. Our deepest fear is that we are powerful beyond measure. It is our light, not our darkness, that most frightens us. We ask ourselves, 'Who am I to be brilliant, gorgeous, talented, and fabulous?' Actually, who are you not to be?"

MARIANNE WILLIAMSON, spiritual teacher and author

Oftentimes we believe we aren't worthy of a wonderful and beautiful life. We doubt ourselves, and think we deserve less than what we're capable of. Stop it. You are capable of so much more.

Instead of thinking about why you shouldn't have what you want, think of all of the reasons why you *do* deserve everything you dream of and more. Write all of these reasons on the following page, and the next time you find yourself feeling unworthy of something, refer back to this list to remind yourself of why you *do* deserve it!

STRIKE A POSE

Have you ever heard of a "Power Pose"? A Power Pose is a strong stance that has been psychologically proven to improve confidence. Try some of the Power Poses here and on the next page for two minutes each, and see which ones help improve your overall self-confidence the most. Practice a favorite pose every morning, or before something nerve-wracking like a presentation or job interview. See just how much of a confidence boost it can give you in the heat of the moment!

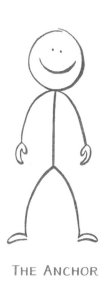

THE ANCHOR

THE SUPERHERO

THE VICTOR

THE CEO

THE REPRESENTATIVE

SHUT DOWN YOUR INNER CRITIC

When you're struggling with self-doubt, it's easy to believe that you should feel bad about yourself. You often believe that you don't deserve happiness, but this couldn't be further from the truth.

Next time you think you don't deserve to feel awesome, stand in front of a mirror, look yourself in the eye, and say: "I deserve happiness." Say it over and over until you believe it. Use conviction, and don't allow your inner critic to argue otherwise—just keep interrupting that negative voice with this phrase until it gives up. Practice this each day until you truly *feel* that you deserve to be happy.

FACE YOUR FEARS

"Everything you want is on the other side of fear."

JACK CANFIELD, author and motivational speaker

Do you find yourself making excuses for not following your dreams or doing something a little different because you're scared?

The images here represent common fears many people experience. Label each image with something that scares you. After, write down ways you can face those fears in the corresponding lines. Next time you're experiencing one of these fears, remember your list and tackle the fear head-on with more confidence than you've ever had before!

FEARS   HOW TO CONQUER

FILL IN
YOUR DESTINY

Job interviews, presentations, and first dates are some of the most nerve-wracking experiences, and they can easily shake your confidence if you don't feel certain of your approach. One great approach is to write out different scenarios and predict how you'll respond to tough situations or questions!

There are three comic strips here. In each comic, there are two figures: one figure already has its speech bubble filled in with an intimidating question. In the blank speech bubble above the second figure (that's you!), write your response to the question and finish the comic like the awesome boss you are!

FIRST DATE

ASKING FOR A RAISE

EMBRACE YOUR PASSIONS

Do you ever feel embarrassed to express your passions? Have you ever shown a lot of excitement for something, only to receive a look from someone that says, "What on earth are you doing? This is weird." If you're not expressing your passions, you are denying the beautiful parts of who you are. In fact, despite the "Negative Nancys" who love to judge others for their passions simply because they don't understand, many people enjoy listening to others express excitement about something—and it often leads to discovering a similar interest. In the space provided, write about anything that sparks excitement in your life. It can be something related to your job, someone you know, a hobby you enjoy—anything!

On the other hand, is there anything in your life that you feel is lacking passion or excitement?

Look at your responses to the first question. What are some ways that you can bring these passions into the parts of your life that you mentioned in the second question? How can you uplift these unpassionate parts of your life to make them more exciting and fulfilling?

Focus on what you enjoy, and don't be afraid to express yourself along the way! After all, these are important parts of what makes you incredibly awesome.

PUT DOWN THE PHONE

When you're spending so much time on social media, you may find yourself comparing your life to the lives you see online. Cutting back on your social media usage will help, but do you know exactly how much time you spend scrolling through media feeds and subconsciously comparing yourself each day?

Throughout the next full week, keep track of how much time you spend on social media each day. You can either check the clock when you start and finish using these apps or social websites; use a timer; or download an app such as AntiSocial or RescueTime that will automatically track how much you use certain apps throughout the day. Use the following chart to log the time spent on these accounts each day of the week. We've provided space to track five accounts, but you can fill fewer columns or add more depending on how many media accounts you use.

TIME SPENT ON SOCIAL MEDIA

DAY	MINUTES ON ACCOUNT #1	MINUTES ON ACCOUNT #2	MINUTES ON ACCOUNT #3	MINUTES ON ACCOUNT #4	MINUTES ON ACCOUNT #5
MONDAY					
TUESDAY					
WEDNESDAY					
THURSDAY					
FRIDAY					
SATURDAY					
SUNDAY					

Now that you've tracked a full week of your social media usage, are you surprised with the results? Do you spend more or less time on these accounts than you thought?

. . . .

What are some activities you can partake in besides scrolling through social media feeds? Brainstorm ideas for activities that will enrich you and help you feel great, instead of feeling less than your awesome self.

TAKE A LEAP OF FAITH

"The hardest step she ever took
was to blindly trust in who she was."

ATTICUS, philosopher

It's time to trust yourself. Close your eyes and
envision yourself living your dream life. Then bring that
image to life in the space provided. You can either
doodle a scene, write out a description, or do a mix of
both! It may not be pretty or look perfect, but what
matters is that you tried, and taking action is better
than being "perfect."

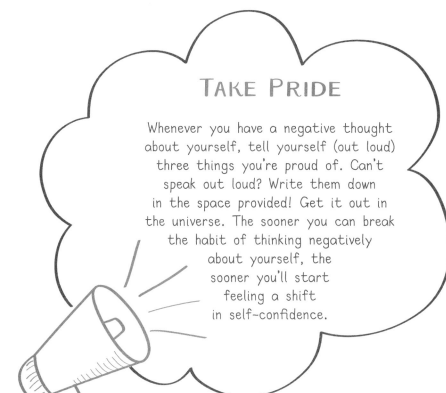

TAKE PRIDE

Whenever you have a negative thought
about yourself, tell yourself (out loud)
three things you're proud of. Can't
speak out loud? Write them down
in the space provided! Get it out in
the universe. The sooner you can break
the habit of thinking negatively
about yourself, the
sooner you'll start
feeling a shift
in self-confidence.

MAKE IT A HABIT

When you struggle to develop or maintain healthy, regular habits that help you achieve your goals, it has a direct effect on how you feel about yourself. Think about how incredible it feels when you create awesome habits that allow you to achieve your goals: it's truly the best! However, building a new habit is a challenging task when you're already dealing with all of life's responsibilities.

Create a schedule for how you spend a typical day. If your weekends are different from your weekdays, or you have specific priorities on certain days, create a schedule for each day. Include how much time you spend on each errand or activity. Be honest with yourself; if you spend a few hours watching a TV show or playing a game on your phone, include it! It's important to have an accurate depiction of how you spend your average day.

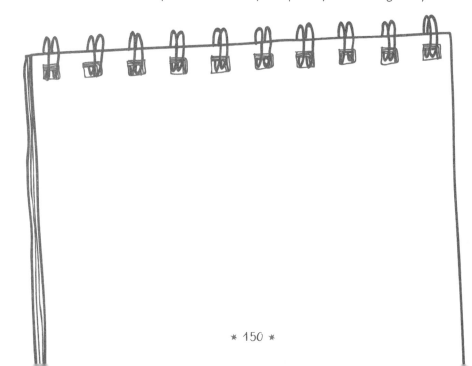

Now that you have a representation of your typical day, is there any room to cut down on certain activities to make space for building a new habit? While it's important to have downtime to relax and recharge, you'd be surprised by how easy it is to add just ten to twenty minutes of time to your schedule dedicated to developing a new habit. Use the space here to write down places where you can make cuts in your day.

When are you going to start implementing this time for your new habit? Be specific!

FUEL YOUR FIRE

*"Be fearless in the pursuit
of what sets your soul on fire."*

UNKNOWN

What sets your soul on fire? What are you doing to include these things in your awesome life? You can use the space here to explore these questions.

LET GO OF PERFECTION

Perfection is an impossible goal. Absolutely nothing will ever be completely flawless in your life. No project, vacation, activity, person—anything. Struggling with perfection is a trap for consistent disappointment in yourself. When you set unrealistically high expectations for yourself, you feel ashamed and crushed when you can't reach these insane goals.

It's time to end that cycle. It's time for you to learn how to move forward with things before they're completely "ready." In order to do so, you first need to reflect on your usual process when working toward a goal. In the space provided, write down this process. How much time do you spend on research, planning, editing, etc.?

Have you ever spent so much time overplanning that you hardly had any time left to actually execute your plan? What were you working on, and how did it play out?

Reflect on your answers, and start practicing taking action *before* things are your version of "perfect." Remember: put in your best effort every time, but stop attempting to achieve unrealistic goals. The more you focus on completing tasks and projects with realistic expectations, the more confident you'll feel in yourself and your abilities!

OWN YOUR OPINIONS

A small, yet powerful step you can take in building your self-confidence and feeling all-around awesome is to start noticing how you present yourself vocally to others. When you pitch an idea at work, do you start with an uncertain tone of, "I'm not sure about this, but..." or, "This might be okay, but what about..." This may seem like a minor detail, but the way you verbally express yourself and your ideas is incredibly important in elevating your own self-confidence and showing others that you believe in what you are saying.

Read through the following example phrases and note which ones exude confidence versus uncertainty.

▶ Our team needs to focus on productivity right now above all else in order to reach our goals for the year.

▶ I suggest we travel to Bali this year. The gorgeous sights and adventures for this affordable price are hard to beat!

▶ I could be completely off base, but maybe we could try a new restaurant downtown that I think I read about the other day?

Which sentence didn't display confidence? If you said the third sentence, then you're right!

You can sense the uncertainty and nervousness with, "I could be completely off base..." and, "maybe...I think..." Imagine you are deciding on a place to eat with friends and someone says this sentence, while another friend says, "Let's go to this amazing restaurant down the street!" Who would you agree with?

In the scenarios here, write down how you would typically present your question or response, without paying attention to your words. Then, look over what you wrote and notice if there are any parts that don't portray confidence. Rewrite these phrases in a more confident manner, and remember this exercise in your daily life!

•••

SCENARIO ONE: You're in a meeting with your team at work, and your boss asks for ideas on how to pitch a new service to a potential client. You raise your hand and say:

•••

SCENARIO TWO: Your class is involved in a group debate project about the importance of alternative energy uses in helping save the planet. A very outspoken member of your group loves to contribute, but many of her ideas are inaccurate and will lead to losing the debate. How do you pitch a better idea?

LEND YOUR SUPPORT

Supporting others in their goals is a
fantastic way to not only help someone achieve
their dreams, but also feel awesome for making
a positive difference!

Have you ever helped someone achieve a goal? Write
about how you helped them in the space provided.

Is there anyone else in your life that you can assist in
accomplishing their dreams? If so, who? And what are some
steps you can take to help them reach their goal?

Reflect on everything you wrote. Look at what you brain-
stormed and how you helped someone accomplish something amazing. You believe that these people can accomplish anything with a
little bit of help and determination. So why can't you have the
same belief in yourself? You deserve your dreams! It's time to
believe in yourself in the same way you believe in others. Use the
same brainstorming process to figure out steps you can take to
reach your own goals.

TREASURE YOUR TRIBE

"Stick to the people who pull the magic out of you, not the madness."

UNKNOWN

Guess what? You have the freedom to pick who you keep in your life. Who are the people who help you feel good and capable of doing anything? Who can you always rely on when life throws its curveballs? These are the people you want to keep in your life. Hold them close, cherish them, and thank them for helping you shine brighter every time you're together.

REFLECT ON YOUR MOTIVATIONS

Do you find yourself overworked and ultimately never left feeling fulfilled? Many people who experience a lot of self-doubt are constantly on the move because they're seeking validation from external sources instead of within themselves. Seeking this kind of external satisfaction and approval will never lead to true self-confidence: how can you tell yourself that you're awesome when you wait for others to tell you first?

Whether you believe that your motivations are from external sources or not, it's important to reflect on *why* you're working toward each of your goals. On the following page, write down all of your goals in the left-hand column: long-term, short-term, big, small—anything that you're work-ing toward in your life. In the right-hand column, write down who you're working toward this goal for. Are each of your goals truly for yourself? Or are some of them more for the approval or validation of someone else?

GOAL ⋮ WHO IS IT FOR?

HOW MANY OF YOUR GOALS ARE FOR OTHER PEOPLE? Is there a way you can reframe these goals so they are for yourself? If you can't find an internal purpose behind some of these goals, don't be afraid to cross them out. Your personal satisfaction and validation will give you a much more authentic sense of confidence in the long run!

REVISIT CHILDHOOD ASPIRATIONS

What are some of the dreams and goals you had as a child? No matter how crazy they may have been (think owning a pizza unicorn or building a rocket to Mars), list or draw them in the space provided!

WHICH OF THOSE DREAMS DO YOU STILL HAVE TODAY? WHY DID YOU MOVE ON FROM THE OTHERS?

If you gave up on any dreams because they felt too "out there," but are still in the realm of possibility (sorry, pizza unicorns), maybe it's time to rethink your reasoning. If a dream is something you're still interested in, give it another try!

REMEMBER
THERE'S NO SHAME
WHEN YOU TRY

When you're working toward a goal, you may feel like no matter how hard you try, you keep missing the mark. It's imperative to remember that if you're trying your best, then you're well on your way to success! There's no shame in giving your best effort. Not sure if you truly are giving it your all? Use the following space to jot out every step you are taking toward your goal, then look over your list to gain perspective on how hard you are trying to succeed. If you decide that you really can do more to reach your goal, use the remaining space to brainstorm ways you can take things up a notch.

TACKLE THE "BIG THREE"

A key step toward feeling awesome about yourself is working on the following:

1. Your thoughts.   2. Your attitude.   3. Your behavior.

These are the three key parts of who you are. Your thoughts determine your beliefs and how you view what you experience each day. Your attitude shapes how you feel about yourself and everything around you. Lastly, your behavior has a direct impact on how you treat yourself and others.

These three elements are also all connected. In fact, if you focus on one of them, you'll actually impact the other two as well. For example, if you start with changing your behavior, employing the "Fake It 'Til You Make It" method of self-confidence, you'll notice a change in your attitude as well, as you begin to feel happier and more confident. This will also shift your thoughts toward positivity and pride in who you are and what you can accomplish.

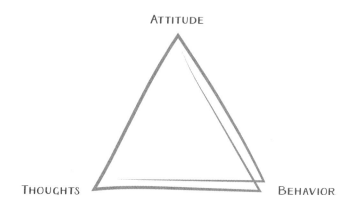

ATTITUDE

THOUGHTS   BEHAVIOR

In order to boost your self-confidence, which part of the dynamic trio do feel you need to work on the most?

Starting with the part you need to work on most, what changes are you going to make in order to kick off your awesome transformation?

Once you've decided what part you're going to start changing and how, solely focus on this first shift. When you focus on the first goal you have created, you'll start to feel that automatic shift within the other two facets. You may not even notice it's happening, but soon enough, you'll start to feel *awesome!*

BRAG A LITTLE

For some reason, people often find themselves embarrassed to speak positively about their traits, talents, and achievements with others. They're usually worried that they'll come off as having a big ego or as bragging about themselves. As a result, they end up hiding their full potential and how awesome they truly are.

This isn't right. You deserve to feel proud and talk about your awesome personal traits, talents, and achievements!

How do you usually feel when you talk positively about yourself to other people?

WHY DO YOU THINK YOU FEEL THIS WAY?

In what ways can you change your mindset about feeling this way? Remember: this is a no-judgment zone. No one is criticizing you or thinking negatively about you. Write down absolutely *everything* you feel and own what makes you incredibly *awesome*. No restrictions, no rules.

SATISFY YOUR
PERSONAL CARE NEEDS

Self-care is an extremely important part of feeling awesome about yourself. Fill the jar with easy ways to take care of yourself. They can be anything from taking five minutes to meditate, going on a walk, or journaling! Include everything that helps you feel refreshed, recharged, and ready to take on your awesome life. Practice at least one of these activities each day.

You can also take this a step further by buying an actual jar to fill with self-care ideas. Whenever you feel stressed or need a break, pick a random activity out of the jar and do what it says!

CELEBRATE YOU!

When you celebrate the small accomplishments you achieve while striving for a larger goal, it can help keep you motivated, excited, and proud of yourself and what you can do! Here are some ideas you can use to celebrate the small wins in your daily life:

DO A VICTORY DANCE IN YOUR ROOM TO YOUR FAVORITE SONG.

TREAT YOURSELF TO YOUR FAVORITE FOOD.

GRAB A DRINK WITH A FRIEND.

GIVE YOURSELF A BREAK AND REST—YOU DESERVE IT!

ENJOY YOUR WEEKEND

In the space provided, describe your ideal Saturday. How do you enjoy spending your time? Are you with friends, enjoying some much-needed alone time, or partaking in your favorite hobbies? Describe your perfect day in as much detail as possible, then turn to the following page.

Are you currently incorporating any of these activities into your day? If not, why? You deserve to have a fantastic weekend that helps you feel awesome and on top of the world. Incorporate at least one of these things into your next day off and see how it feels!

REFRAME REJECTION

One of the strongest blows to self-confidence is rejection. The pain and embarrassment you experience when you're rejected can seem insurmountable in the moment. However, many people don't realize that rejections aren't necessarily endings, but redirections to where you're meant to go. For example, a closed door for a career opportunity could actually redirect you toward an even better job the following week. A brutal breakup creates the opportunity to meet someone new who may in fact be a better fit for you. With this in mind, the best way to handle rejection is to focus on what you can accomplish now that that door has been closed.

In the following space, reflect back on one or two of the toughest rejections that you've endured, then turn to the next page for more guidance. What doors unexpectedly shut down your original plans?

HOW DID YOU FEEL WHEN YOU RECEIVED THE NEWS
ABOUT THESE REJECTIONS?

WHAT OPPORTUNITIES APPEARED AFTER THE
REJECTIONS?

WHERE DID THESE NEW DIRECTIONS LEAD YOU?

The next time you receive a rejection, remind yourself
that you're simply meant for a more awesome opportunity!

REFLECT ON YOUR ABUNDANCE

An important part of feeling awesome about yourself is focusing on what you have, rather than what you don't have. It's easy to spend your time thinking about what you want or need (especially when other people have those things), rather than feeling grateful for what you already have in your life.

Use the space provided to write down all of the awesome things that you have in your life. The next time you start feeling jealous or disappointed about what you don't have, refer back to this page to remind yourself that you have an abundant life. Remember, someone out there is jealous of *you* and wishing that he or she had *your* life!

WRITE A
SELF-LOVE LETTER

Write a love letter to yourself on a separate piece of paper. Include every single thing you love about yourself. Don't hold back! When you're finished, fold this letter and have someone else hide it somewhere you will find as a surprise later. Brighten your future self's day!

APPENDIX:
ADDITIONAL RESOURCES

This section includes recommended additional books, websites, blogs, and empowering songs to help you feel even more awesome throughout your incredible self-confidence journey. Combining these resources with the work you've accomplished in this book, you're well on your way to being the best and most beautiful version of yourself that you can possibly be!

BOOKS

You Are a Badass by Jen Sincero

Playing Big by Tara Mohr

Girl, Wash Your Face by Rachel Hollis

Big Magic by Elizabeth Gilbert

Awaken the Giant Within by Tony Robbins

WEBSITES AND BLOGS

Sara Katherine
Sara-Katherine.com

Life with Confidence
www.life-with-confidence.com

Psychology Today
www.psychologytoday.com/us/basics/confidence

Self-Confidence.co.uk
www.self-confidence.co.uk

PODCASTS

The Goal Digger Podcast by Jenna Kutcher

Pursuit with Purpose Podcast by Melyssa Griffin

RISE Podcast by Rachel Hollis

The Lavendaire Lifestyle by Aileen Xu

SELF-CONFIDENCE PLAYLIST

"Confident" by Demi Lovato

"Unstoppable" by Sia

"Do My Thing" by Estelle feat. Janelle Monáe

"Not Afraid" by Eminem

"Run the World (Girls)" by Beyoncé

"Rule the World" by Walk Off the Earth

"Just Fine" by Mary J. Blige

"I Won't Back Down" by Tom Petty and the Heartbreakers

"Love Myself" by Hailee Steinfeld

"Titanium" by David Guetta feat. Sia

"Born This Way" by Lady Gaga

"Don't Stop Me Now" by Queen

"Stronger (What Doesn't Kill You)" by Kelly Clarkson

"Roar" by Katy Perry

"Brave" by Sara Bareilles

About the Author

SARA KATHERINE is a writer, blogger, and marketing manager. After publishing her first book, *Sara Earns Her Ears*, she launched her current personal development blog, Sara-Katherine.com, where she strives to help empower millennials to find their passions and live their best lives. Her work appears on Amendo.com and *The Sophisticated Gal*. Born and raised in California, Sara also loves Disney, Marvel movies, and her cat, Mochi.